Red Dirt Revival:
a poetic memoir in 6 Breaths

Expanded Second Edition

Tim'm T. West

Praise for *Red Dirt Revival*

Courage of form, courage of content. Sensuous thinking. Radical motion. Tim'm T. West carries forward Audre Lorde's practice of poetry as the "light by which we scrutinize our lives." With its embrace-critique of origins and its bravura leap from academic precincts into vernacular revelation, this book renews my hope for our collective survival.
— Jan Clausen, author of *Apples and Oranges: My Journey Through Sexual Identity*

The writer descends onto us directly from Foucault's dream; an intellectual destroyer of evidence and universalities who locates the weak points of a trembling building. Tim'm West is a construction worker incessantly displacing himself in a backwoods called America. Here, West romantically girds himself with the language of memory and insurgent impatience; words too vital to be the stuff of cute couplets and rhyme schemes—these tools are more than operatives, hewing the joists of critical observation to the slats of personal testimony. If West can't see the strength of tomorrow, it's only because his eyes are so fiercely fastened to locating now.
— Carl Hancock Rux, author of *Pagan Operetta and Asphalt*

In this collection of stories, Tim'm T. West is the harvest part of love and writing that Essex Hemphill and Assotto Saint sowed, knowing that from some red-dirt somewhere, some new bloom, some man-child Tim'm, would claim his place as griot, next in our broken royal line. Surely what grows from red dirt is what nourishes us, gives us life— gives us love.
— Marvin K. White, author of *Last Rights* and *nothin' ugly fly*

I read a lot of poetry—and some of it takes root in my brain, stays with me for days, visiting my mouth in odd moments and making me speak it into whatever room I'm in at the time. Tim'm West's incredible, affecting extraordinary works, as rooted in rhythm as a heartbeat, as vital as the blood it pumps, seem to stand up and shout from the pages. A poetic memoir about growing up black and gay in lower Arkansas, *Red Dirt Revival* . . . sings. There's just no other word for it. It sings a full-throated song, and if you have an ounce of music in your soul, you'll want to listen a long time.
— S Bear Bergman, author of *Butch is a Noun*

Red Dirt Revival is a multifarious body of work that is as exacting and poignant as it is breathtaking. My psyche and my emotions are still trying to catch their collective breath.
— Antonio Le Mons, author of *How To Ruin The Perfect Child*

A founding member of the "Homo-Hop" group Deepdickollective, Tim'm West is almost dizzyingly multitalented. . . . *Red Dirt Revival* mixes poetry and prose in a way reminiscent of Essex Hemphill's collection *Ceremonies* to chart his life from growing up poor and abused in Arkansas to eventual self-acceptance and pride as an HIV+ out gay man. While one can chart the influence of other writers, both gay and straight, black and white, in his work, West again and again proves himself to be very much his own man: proud, defiant, Southern. His language shows him to be equally at home on the streets as well as in the halls of academe.
— Reginald Harris, author of *Ten Tongues: Poems*

With courage and optimism Tim'm West offers students a compelling testimony of crafting self and community in the face of physical and representational violence. A brilliant addition to any course addressing identity, resistance and the politics and poetics of representation.
— Dr. Kim Berry, Chair, Department of Critical Race, Gender and Sexuality Studies, Humboldt State University

Unlike many other reviewers of this volume, I'm a lousy poetry reader. As an analyst and dealer in ideas, I often miss images and nuances of poetry. And that's probably why I enjoy Tim'm West's poetry—he leaps from idea to image and back again, to show me both the ideas and the experience he evokes in this volume. The work, while mysterious and exciting, is quite accessible; I don't need a degree in literary theory to get it. West offers a passport that allows me to visit a life I can never experience, and through it, see a humanity common to us all.
— Dr. Das Janssen, Assistant Professor of Philosophy, Chicago State University

Acknowledgements/Inspirations

There is much that I could say about each of you, still with me, even those who left their spirits behind to guide. In these pages, somewhere between the beginning of an emotion and a period, you are remembered.

To Ayanna U'Dongo for resuscitation at the pivotal point at which this book was conceptualized and for, a decade later, reminding me to keep breathing.

A'shar Mitchell. With you came inspiration beyond this book. Thanks for your support in the writing of this book and for your faith in me as a writer and change agent, beyond the first edition. Still a friend of mine.

Thanks to my first edition Red Dirt Revival production team: Marian O'Brien of Boku Books for all of your savvy in the art of publishing and for demonstrating that RDR's resonance has no bounds. And to Mai-Lei Pecorari of Redefine Design for honoring the breath of my work with imagery and a cover that captured its sensuality.

Thanks to the team who've worked to bring the 2nd Edition of this book to life, ten years after its debut: Christina Accomando, for honoring your own introduction to *Red Dirt Revival* by Eric Rofes, who believed greatly in my work. Our continuing friendship is a testament to the amazing man he remains in the hearts of so many. Karla Rivas, for being present, amid your own life's struggles, to extend this poetic memoir to people who, like you, may be moved to tell their own truths. Briian Dargon for many reasons to smile, not the least of which is the magic you provide as a photographer. Thanks for honoring, still, Mai-Lei's original design in your rendition of the cover. Truitt O'Neal for 11th hour Graphic Design consultation. You've been far more than a manager or friend. Many times over you've been my own personal superman. Thank you. Thanks also to Darnell for being not only a scholar attuned to the power of praxis, but also a model for what the work represents, in more ways than one.

Dixons, Stinsons, and Wests everywhere. My daughter Shannon Matesky, Antione Blakley (for being a rock for me), Keith Jaki' Arrington (for lessons in friendship), Marvin K. White, Michael Smith, Jan Clausen, Samantha Chang, Carl Hancock Rux, members of Deep Dickollective (Juba, JB, Marcus, Ralowe, Phil, Doug E. Dazié,

ButtaFlySoul, Ry, Baraka Noe, SoulNubian), Anthony Gibson, B.J. Samuels, Vincent Holmes, Bryant Davis, Byron "August" Oakman, Louie Butler, Chris Bostic, James "Belasco" Tucker, Bay Watson, Carlos Gardinet, Derrick Pinkney, Jermaine Smith, Jackie Wigfall, Cher McCallister, Shelton "Chad" Wallace, Gloria Anzaldúa, Audre Lorde, Hélène Cixous, Darrell Bogan, DJ David Harness, Greg Millet, Monica Young, Gerald Todd, Alice Walker, James Hardy, E. Lynn Harris, Marlon Riggs, Melvin Dixon, Joseph Beam, Essex Hemphill, Jupiter, staff who supported me through my time at SMAAC Youth Center, the Church of Jesus Christ of Latter Day Saints, Phillip Atiba Goff, Broderick Harrison, James Dorsey, Darryl Pope, Michael Ali, Hanifah Walidah, DJ So Much Soul, Saul Williams, Martin Luther, Ledisi, Greg Tate, Robert Hardy, Salman Rushdie, Cherríe Moraga, Stanford Program in Modern Thought and Literature, Sharon Holland, Harry Elam, Maureen Cullins, Corey Courts, Debbie and Maisha Smart, Duke University Class of 1994, Howard University, The New School for Social Research, Amala Levine, Steve Caton, Terry Williams, Dom Apollon, Kyla Wazana, Ife Udoh, Lance McCready, Greg O'Neal Miller, Goddrick Austin, Matthew Kyle, Black Gay Letter and Arts Movement (BGLAM), Kolo Wamba, Sarah Dodds, Angie Harris, Michel Foucault, Gilles Deleuze, James Baldwin, Freekanos, Anthony Appiah, Alexis "Promise" Smith, Black Dot Collective, Mignon Freeman, Oakland School for the Arts and all the amazing artists and writers I taught there, Earl Fowlkes, Cesar Chavez Public Charter School for Public Policy, College Summit, Inc., AID Atlanta and Deeper Love Project, Humboldt State University Critical Race, Gender, and Sexuality Studies Department (CRGS), St. Hope Foundation, Houston Community College, Center on Halsted, L. Michael Gipson, Ken J. Martin, Aubrey Moultry, Black Alphabet Film Festival family, Sonya Renee, Karen Ladson, Marc Bamuthi Joseph, Nhojj, Roy Kinsey, CC Carter and POW WOW, E. Patrick Johnson, Byron Hurt, Mario Van Peebles, James Peterson, Tobias Spears, Eric "Caddy" Watkins, Eddy J. Free & Steve Harris, Kevin Taylor, Joan Morgan, April Preyer, Nancy Olson, Pam Iverson, Ricky Talley, Tonya Netjes, Regina Bradley, Mark Anthony Neal, Eric Commodore, Jay Torrence, Ron Taylor, Jr., Brian D. Zarley, Julius D. Bailey, Ken Like Barbie, Johnny Mitchell (HHH), Christopher Wimbley, Gil Shannon, Ann Kenner, Doffie Camper, colleagues and youth at Center on Halsted, and countless others who are remembered because they remember that it was not my intent to forget them. Thank you.

Dedications

she who elicits the song of a thousand butterflies
is the angel who will guide my pen.
after I have shined the barrel of her mama's gun
it is her strength I will pray for.
my siren song experiences her reverb—
courage crying for keys to heaven,
a smile,
flowers that grow in concrete jungles.
she has whispered a reminder that
boys like me are nothing less than a diamond—
a coal under pressure
made more precious
with every heart-hurt
every mis-trial or -ism.
her shine sneaks inside of raindrops
each one matching a rhythm
waiting to be danced—
forming a tear-stream awaiting its redemption,
like a pen eclipsing a poem
or a next breath.

I think of you and am reminded: "Diamonds are coals under pressure"

Charlette Latrice West, Irma Pearl Stinston, Ellen Dixon-Stinson
My brothers (Joseph, Matthew, David, Charles Everick) and my
brothas, my sisters (Felicia, Toya, Talisha, Stephanie) and sistahs,
Corey Williams, Corey Courts, Eric Rofes, Steve Williams,
Kaya Nati, Rickey Williams, Brandon Lacy Campos, for Dad who has
taught me most about how to live, and for Venus Opal Reese for shar-
ing with me the "Breath" of her work.

Contents

Red Dirt Revival

a poetic memoir in 6 Breaths

Introduction to the Second Edition

"Wanna make me a better body": Disidentification and Radical
Imagination in the Breaths of Tim'm T. West

By Christina Accomando

With unflinching analysis *and* unabashed hope, Tim'm T. West forges
links between poetry and prose, academia and activism, hip hop and
feminism, the red dirt of Arkansas and the academic halls of Stan-
ford—modeling what is possible when we dare to connect across
differences, willing to be surprised by who our allies might be. Speak-
ing in multiple voices—Black queer positive / country city university /
teacher poet scholar MC / brave and vulnerable—West makes audible
the contradictions and confluences of our lives, by examining vividly
the complexities of his own multiple identities.

As a black, queer, masculine-identified pro-feminist poet, academic
and hip hop artist, Tim'm West has numerous identities to negotiate. In
the face of violence or injustice, we often try to take refuge in an iden-
tity that might offer a community of support and resistance. Not unlike
Audre Lorde finding herself both a sister *and* outsider in relation to the
diverse groups to which she belonged, again and again West finds
himself connected to *and* alienated from his multiple communities. So
"identity" in his work often means something more like
"disidentification"—feeling both a part of and rejected by an individu-
al or community, neither fully assimilating nor fully opposing the
identity. José Esteban Muñoz offers this understanding of the term:

> Disidentification is meant to be descriptive of the survival
> strategies the minority subject practices in order to negotiate a
> phobic majoritarian public sphere that continuously elides or
> punishes the existence of subjects who do not conform to the
> phantasm of normative citizenship. (4)

For West, that "majoritarian public sphere" can also be embodied by a
minority within which he is a more marginalized minority—a queer
citizen in hip hop nation, for example.

Identity and imagination are linked in West's writing and can mean
imagining radical new identities—alternative masculinities, different
notions of Blackness, new ideas about love—and messy coalition
spaces of multiple and unexpected identities coming together. West
also finds he must imagine new genres to contain (or at least encircle)

these multitudes. *Red Dirt Revival: a poetic memoir in 6 Breaths*, as the subtitle suggests, stirs into its mix poetry, memoir, letters, theory, rap, spoken word, and more. And in West's hands each of these elements is more complicated than we might imagine. Poetic memoir both draws upon experience *and* creates something new. "The farthest horizons of our hopes and fears," writes Audre Lorde, "are cobbled by our poems, carved from the rock experiences of our daily lives." In her essay "Poetry is Not a Luxury," Lorde counters the forces that dismiss creativity in general and poetry in particular as an unnecessary adjunct to the real work of rationality and literalness, arguing instead that poetry is "a vital necessity of our existence." Poetry also can allow us to imagine—and enact—something new: "It forms the quality of the light within which we predicate our hopes and dreams toward survival and change, first made into language, then into idea, then into more tangible action" (37). If we think of poetry as a luxury, as ivory tower contemplation, it's the opposite of action, but Lorde sees a direct line from creative language to tangible action, from dreams to survival.

The survival articulated in *Red Dirt Revival* is in the face of not only society's racism and homophobia but also intolerance and violence in our most intimate spaces—in the family, within one's community, within oneself.

In grappling with a complex father figure, West challenges the violence of domestic abuse and gender policing through fearless truth-telling *and* the narration of alternative masculinities. In "body talk" he writes about witnessing, trying to interrupt, and continuing to resist the legacies of a father's violence. The speaker both recounts and refuses the narratives of violence that shaped his growing up, juxtaposing the disruption of his father's fist and the protection from outside threats offered by his mother. With both critique and love, the speaker analyzes his father's verbal and physical violence as coming not from strength but from his unacknowledged vulnerability: "shouting when he should cry / crushing and sucker-punching his vulnerability / out on mama's mouth."

West also interrogates the relationship between vulnerability and male violence in "About Radicalia Feminista," arguing: "Men cloak the lack with violence. Each time he strikes her body or spirit he is further removed from that frightened boy within himself who fears that his weakness will be uncovered . . . Vulnerability for some boys is such a terrifying bottomless pit that they strike relentlessly at everything, believing that even death and war and the battle scars are better than

living with the 'lack' that is open, fluid, innocent, peaceful . . . is gene-
sis." He reclaims as life-giving this lack that is supposed to be
terrifying, but this reclaiming is not an easy process, particularly with
a father who frequently models violent masculinity.

In "body talk" and in the rest of *Red Dirt Revival* West doesn't com-
pletely reject the father—this tension is part of the complex
relationship of disidentification: "he is not always violent. / sometimes
I think that he is more / handsome than cruel." The speaker reports
contradictory patriarchal commands: "always protect your mama . . .
even against me," and offers an example of rejecting the father's be-
havior even as the son respects his words, once taking a cut from a
knife meant for the mother. The blade "didn't go deep at all / but for-
ever impressed itself / underneath my skin. / did just what daddy told. /
my body protecting her body against his." This is a powerfully con-
crete disidentifying moment—the speaker assimilates his father's
words while rejecting his behavior, and carves an identity out of that
contradiction: the knife doesn't cut deeply *into* his skin, but the mean-
ing of the incident is impressed *under* his skin.

West insists on imagining a different way to be a man, one that em-
bodies both the opposite of paternal violence *and* loving aspects of the
father:

> I contemplated the opposite of hitting
> the opposite of him
> identification with the side of a man
> that dad was most afraid of

Lorde credits poetry with giving "name to the nameless so it can be
thought"—the speaker here doesn't yet have the affirmative name for
"the opposite of hitting" but the mere writing of this poem—rewriting
memory through poetry—begins that process of cobbling something
new (37).

The solution West imagines explicitly involves writing: not silencing
that painful history but finding a different way to remember it—one
that doesn't traumatize—one that cobbles a road in a different direc-
tion:

> trying to write words that resolve
> those living and breathing memories.
> trying to love all our bodies—

> crying in order to erase
> horror-wounds with
> soft-blue pen tears
> years later.
> wanting a body-talk medicine
> that cures remembering
> of its trauma.

Writing can offer healing, through "soft-blue pen tears" and "body-talk medicine." West re-writes not only a personal familial narrative of domestic abuse but also societal notions of masculinity predicated on violence. He disidentifies with the father, connecting to the loving and vulnerable parts that are covered up by brutal heteropatriarchy, sucker-punches, and contradictory messages to his son, who resists sometimes with his body, but also by using poetry to imagine "a better body / than his body." The poem's closing lines look to the speaker's own body as a site of imagining a new identity—beginning to find words and images for what "the opposite" can look like:

> wanna make me a better body
> than his body
> a better body
> a my body   body
> anybody
> can body-love

West cobbles a new word here—the hyphenated "body-love," which is perhaps giving name to the nameless so the "opposite of hitting" can be thought. A body "anybody / can body-love" also points to his imagining an alternative to compulsory heterosexuality and violent heteronormativity.

The first poem in this poetic memoir, "negation," also addresses the poet's contradictory father-son relationship. Here, the speaker considers the father's violent response had he known his seed would spawn a gay son:

> I am certain that he would have spilled it on the ground
> stepped on it and spit on it

and said:
"I WILL NOT HAVE A FAGGOT SON"

Unlike the violence in "body talk," here is an imagined violence—had his father committed this act, the poet wouldn't be here to offer this analysis—and it sets up another moment of disidentification: "I wonder why I still love that man so?" The father is unable to imagine "the beauty . . . and joy" his seed might bring, while the speaker *is* able to imagine how it is precisely through the father's negation that the son is the person he is, including learning from his dad "not to take / too much shit off' anyone, / and to be too proud, too black, / and too strong." The son's ability to take these lessons to heart, even if it means rejecting other aspects of the father, seems related the ability to listen to that contradictory instruction in "body talk" to "always protect your mama . . . even against me." West's "negation" both identifies patriarchal violence, and imagines a way to transform it into love, strength and resistance.

In "unnatural acts" West enlarges his argument from a father's targeted homophobia to the larger societal anxiety of "some" who would sooner witness Black male violence than Black male love:

> . . . some would rather see
> his blakk fist
> smashing teeth
> gum-bleeding   and swollen
> blakk skin
> than witness
> him caressing my hand
> him lovingly stroking my face
> 'cause he felt like it
> that moment
> and could not wait
> for the safety of closed quarters

Public violence is normalized, while public affection between men is rendered "unnatural" as well as unsafe. Each stanza juxtaposes culturally preferred real-life, filmic or hip hop representations of Black men intimately locked in violence set against Black men locked in intimacy, with some points of commonality, like the "amplified heart beating" that can result from acts of violence or love. "I sometimes wonder," the speaker concludes, "which acts some think / are most unnatural":

> blakk life ended
> by the hands of another
> blakk man
> or life
> cradled, kept, cherished
> adored, made   safe.

The vivid descriptions of violence and threats are culturally familiar, while West cobbles something unfamiliar in the equally vivid lines of love, critiquing their construction as "unnatural."

In another piece asking us to imagine something radically new, "Suicide Journal" opens Breath 4: dis/ease. It is a heart-stopping two-page lyrical-prose meditation on death, dis/ease, and strategies for survival, actually composed in a psych ward, when West—after checking himself in—had to wait three days before he was finally allowed a stub of pencil. As he struggles with his own identity in this moment of nearly snuffing it out for good, he also imagines a community more heterogeneous than lines of family or ethnicity alone would produce: "My tribe?" he asks. "We lure Holocausts and Middle Passages and executions and lynchings and rapes because we threaten those who want to promote the idea that heaven is after and not now, up there and not here. We want to make it happen here." This is a violence-packed definition of his people, followed by a more nurturing cross-cultural imagining: "I want to kiss a Korean baby on her forehead and call her my lil' ghetto-daughter, teach a bagpipe player how to accompany a DJ scratch." Here again we sense not only Lorde's notion of naming something to help us imagine it, but also her pairing of fear and hope.

Ultimately this window into madness and sanity calls explicitly for creative expression, a literature that will "create a suicide journal, before the event, that I can read and be afraid of the consequences . . . and not follow through." This most personal of moments becomes a collective call for a literature of survival and resistance: "I want to solicit an army of writing rebels . . . whose optimism and hope for heaven on earth is as sensible as a suicide journal: volatile, full of passion, wishing to be found before the exit, a daily manifesto for salvation." What could have been a devastating story of a 27-year-old on the brink of self-destruction instead becomes an empowering call for creative salvation and allies across differences. West's poem "Litany for Survival"—a title he adapts from Audre Lorde—ends with the line (grammatically a question but with no question mark): "What else is writing / if not evidence of his survival."

When Tim'm West first published *Red Dirt Revival: a poetic memoir in 6 breaths* a decade ago, he was quite literally offering this inspiring (a word that originally meant *to breathe into*) writing as evidence of his survival, in a moment when he did not know his own chances for physical survival. Or, what he did know—with an HIV/AIDS diagnosis and no optimistic prognosis—was not very hopeful. He left a doctoral program at Stanford University and founded Deep Dickollective, not knowing how much time he had, committed to speaking his truth and paying homage to men like Marlon Riggs and Essex Hemphill who paved the way but who also had fewer options for survival. In this 10th Anniversary second edition, the work reappears with as much urgency, with continued relevance, and with the resonance of how much survival has transpired in the last decade.

In addition to the original "6 Breaths," the second edition includes a new section, "Still Breathing," a testament to West's continued survival, productivity and inspiration. Fundamental theoretical pieces, like "Keepin' It Real: Disidentification and its Discontents" (first published in *Black Cultural Traffic*) appear alongside "Killin' Me" (published in a limited edition chapbook *Love in Full Color*, created to raise awareness during the 2008 campaign to defeat California's Proposition 8) and previously performed but never before published pieces (including works from his one-man-show *Ready, Set, Grow*). A particularly salient unpublished work is "prognosis," dedicated to West's father and articulating a complex disidentification that marks father-son relationships throughout his poetic memoir. *Red Dirt Revival*, not surprisingly, is both a classic text and a living, breathing work of art, communication and community. It has meant many things to many readers, from gay Black men West intended to reach and white queer activist/educator Eric Rofes (whose books he had on his shelf, not knowing they would ever meet), to women of color and straight white women he had no idea would be transformed by his words. Students of all ages, cultures and disciplines have discovered his words in ethnic and gender studies, queer theory, literature and cultural studies classes, as well as campus lectures and online videos. It turns out that women, men and youth of all colors, sexualities and geographies find much with which to identify in the words of this blakkboy from the red dirt of Arkansas. These many locations of transformation and inspiration must also be part of the ongoing litany for survival that is Tim'm West's living body of work.

West asks, "What's a blakkboy to do / when his spirit is luring him to write / when there are words stuck in the throat." The rest of his "Litany for Survival" is a litany of obstacles, haltings and silences—"What happens when / alphabets distract / pens bleed"—as well as frustrating and imperfect strategies ("He must read Baraka and Foucault and Genet / until his eyes are so blood-red / that he imagines roses in the margins"). There's no easy answer in this poem, no "well-intentioned savior" who will make "dis/ease" go away, only "the top of a blank page / some lead or ink and his/story to write," and it turns out that is still quite a lot.

Lorde's "A Litany for Survival" is offered for "For those of us who live at the shoreline" and "those of us who were imprinted with fear"—itemizing why the marginalized are afraid to speak, and why, even "when we are silent / we are still afraid." Lorde concludes:

So it is better to speak
remembering
we were never meant to survive

Lorde takes the grim fact of threats to one's survival as an inspirational starting point—if silence in the end does not protect us, then let us speak anyway. Rather than constraining, Lorde's observation is actually liberating. In "Poetry is Not a Luxury," Lorde offers poetry as a response to fear, asserting that "it is the skeleton architecture of our lives. It lays the foundation for a future of change, a bridge across our fears of what has never been before" (38).

If poetry is indeed architecture, what is Tim'm West building in this poetic memoir? I think the answer includes complicated identities and acknowledged disidentifications; communities across differences; and radically different notions of masculinity, sexuality and cultural identity—"a better body" for all of us.

Works Cited:

Lorde, Audre. "A Litany for Survival." *The Black Unicorn*. New York: Norton, 1978.
Lorde, Audre. "Poetry is Not a Luxury." *Sister/Outsider*. Freedom, CA: Crossing Press, 1984.
Muñoz, José Esteban. *Disidentifications: Queers of Color and the Performance of Politics*. Minneapolis: University of Minnesota Press, 1999.

Christina Accomando is a professor of English and Critical Race, Gender & Sexuality Studies at Humboldt State University in Arcata, California. She is the author of *"The Regulations of Robbers": Legal Fictions of Slavery and Resistance* (Ohio State University Press), and her articles have appeared in *Still Seeking an Attitude: Critical Reflections on the Work of June Jordan, Norton Critical Edition of Incidents in the Life of a Slave Girl*, and journals including *MELUS, African American Review, Feminism & Psychology,* and *The Antioch Review*. She was introduced to Tim'm West's work by friend and colleague Eric Rofes, who lent her his copy of *Red Dirt Revival* in 2006, the summer he suddenly died, and she has been teaching it in ethnic studies, women's studies and multicultural queer studies classes ever since.

Introduction to the First Edition

As we travel this world seemingly alone and sometimes lost…barely breathing above raging waves of despair, an extraordinary being appears. In that moment, however long or minute, they bring you clarity, love, hope and guidance. Tim'm West has been that presence in my life, a force of nature—calmly defiant, street-smart and rural-wise.

He's a thick, Black yam, deep-fried Lower Arkansas style; ripened through adversity, dreams and sheer determination. He is a free spirit, a contemplator of his place in this world. He is the midwife whose urban chantings give birth to transformation and healing; calling us to re-think, self-reflect, feel the real.

He is a verbal alchemist, a Barry-toned siren who sings us into tranquilo silence. He is a ravenous scholar, a nationally recognized Homo Hop MC (AKA 25percenter), an HIV activist, freedom fighter and revolutionary poet. He's a masculinity chameleon, a genderbusta, an uncomplicated seductress. He's got school-boy, banjee realness down and Queernation folks lookin' up.

When he requested that I be an editor of this book, I was shocked and deeply honored. As a lover of books and a wanna-be writer, I secretly felt inadequate of such a charge…then I read his life. Each line of his poems, letters and essays revealed layers of a Tim'm I had not known before. To see how he has transcended intense moments of pain, depression, and rejection filled me with enormous courage—he is the bravest person I've ever known. He is my friend…my sistuh-spirit.

Between these sheets are writhing bodies that testify to the power of defiance, survival and passion. With each encounter these double-jointed spirits breathe fire and air into contained live. *Red Dirt Revival* is the celebration of one man's continuous fight to be born again into "personhood" while seeking unconditional love.

As his words reflect his journey, they do not surface from a singular vortex, but are a powerful extremity evolving inside of a collective body—a new generation of voices that speak to the challenges of living in a homophobic, fractured, and frightened society. They speak volumes of tight fits and sheltering shadows while learning to withstand the blisterin' heat of controversy, ignorance and fear.

They are the new Harriet Tubmans, James Baldwins, Cesar Chavezes, Sitting Bulls and Audre Lordes.

Red Dirt Revival is a living testimony. With these six "Breaths" Tim'm West courageously unveils his world to you.[1]

Breath 1: *Front Porches* are the formative years of Tim'm's life, from his rural childhood ("Jacks Crossing") to his submersion into domestic violence in "body talk," and into the challenges of self-actualization through college life.

Breath 2: *Soul Searchin'* is where he confronts the negative aspects of racism and homophobia in socialized practices within black culture. "Soul Unfinished" is a poetic, existential question about blackness and "Gaze on Mandingo," a sampling of how he deploys academic writing to address subject-position, black masculinity, and liberation.

Breath 3: *Queer Rhytes* deals with rites of passage. "Dear Book" is a haunting and candid story of early childhood awareness, "A Letter to Hélène Cixous" pays tribute to one of his most influential womyn writers, and "About Radicalia Feminista" and "Jupiter" trouble our uncomplicated notions of gender socialization.

Breath 4: *Dis/Ease* explores life after HIV, "Iffection," "Letter to Mom," "Ceremonies (for Essex)" and "Suicide Journal" are honest entries into Tim'm's self-discovery after testing HIV positive. Dis/ease for Tim'm marks "opportunity" for a personal sense of Revival.

Breath 5: *Erotiks* is a recollection of fiery passions, broken hearts and quivering possibilities. It's a testament to the gifts dis/ease can bring. In fact, a more eroticized body and mind is the possibility realized through a self-love that he was, perhaps, not aware of prior to testing HIV positive. "Quickie" is a piece some consider Tim'm's signature poem, while "Asskisser," defiant "Thanks" to a (once) homophobic father.

Breath 6: *Dis/Closeur: New Year Revolution, A Ritual Celebrating the Kwanzaa Principle Kuumba (Creativity)* is an open and poignant reve-

---

1 Breath summaries were omitted from the 1st Edition of *Red Dirt Revival* but provide important context in this 2nd Edition. Breaths 1-6 remain the same as the 1st edition, save copyedits, to preserve the fidelity of the original work. Breath 7 contains work the editorial team believed to be critical to a larger body of work beyond Tim'm's "Dis/Closeur" (Breath 6)

lation, a proclamation of self-acceptance, self-love, and promise for a full-life ahead.

As you read *Red Dirt Revival*—as you breathe with it—draw enough courage and boldness to seek your own truths...fearlessly and with conviction.

Ayanna U'Dongo
2002

Ayanna U'Dongo is a practicing Menea (urban sexual shaman), artist/teacher, photographer, sex educator, writer and independent video artist. Her tenacious evolution as a self-trained independent video artist began in the 1990s while on staff at Video Data Bank, a Chicago-based independent video distributorship. U'Dongo "re-appropriates" classic film and television footage to explore sexuality, gender, erotic pleasure, cultural identity and personal power in Post-Slavery America (PSA). Her signature video, *Edges* (1992), has screened in numerous venues in the U.S. and internationally; other videoworks are *Moon Song of the Nubiánts* (1993), *Passion/Fruit & Whisperings* (1996), and *Aborigitron: Affairs of the Hybrid Heart* (2000), which was accepted at the Whitney Museum 2000 Biennial Exhibition in New York City. U'Dongo is developing a semi-biographical video series entitled *Cobalt Chronicle Blues* and writing two neo-fantasy stories, *Fourth Eye of Ja'DoQuil* and *Shivers Reign*. U'Dongo currently resides in Northern California.

Breath 1

Front Porches

Jacks Crossing

Where I come from there is a long winding road a few years old paved. Before we moved there, it was just dirt, red and brown; and the thick of it use'ta make us little dusty, corn-fed kids choke on long walks after oil trucks passed. There is this one road in particular, endless and slick from the droppings of industrialization. On its sides are tall green pine. Now half the pine is gone. The breeze does not carry their scent. At Jacks Crossing, three miles south of Taylor, Arkansas (population 657), the rich inherit their loot, the middle class are really working class, and the others just scratch and scrub floors, bale hay, and work at the chicken plant for groceries to feed the babies they keep making. In Taylor, and more so on the out-skirts, there don't seem to be much else to do but work and fight to make babies and survive. Politics at the White House ain't ever gave two shits about our Black Belt except for its cash crops. Ironic, since Mr. Clinton come from them parts. In the Black Belt towns have small names: Hope, Stamps, Buckner, Emerson. There are just black people and white people who mistrust and hate each other, or who push their hearts to reconcile. But it's kinda hard for heart-strings to meet halfway at the tracks for fear of a choo-choo coming and obstructing the dialogue.

Where I come from children look forward to trips to the county seat and Wal-Mart: It is our mall; and McDonalds, the high school hangout. Where I'm from there is a different kind of ghettofabulousness—some call it dirty dirty South . . . Souf spelled with an "f." I just say that these are the blackest parts of the earth out-side Africa herself. Many niggas where I come from are forgotten; so I'm pushing myself to remember boomboxes placed just inside of rust-ed screen windows to catch the latest R&B croons while mowing the field, shootin' hoops, or digging the next shithole.

Somewhere in this here present, there is a voice I want to call up and country names I want to sound out. I want to let the edges of these sounds resonate in my throat. I want to hear the rhythm that is the gen-esis of B-bonics—code words that deny the irrational faculties of slave catchers, blood, or crips. I want to remember Junior High School crushes on Mike Jones—bow legged and thick lipped. I used to throw him ally-oops and watch his hands caress the ball: Beautiful! He made me understand myself better 'cause at practice I would purposely bump into his blackbody sweat. I'd take a charge and await his country

blackboy care: "You ahhite, nigga? He'd ask. "Yeah I'm cool," I'd re-
ply. And I was.

I remember Zapp and Roger and Nucleas and the synthesized voice
box screaming: "I, I wanna be your man. . . I, I wanna be your man." I
remember contemporary juke joints like the Oasis Club and slow jams
with women whose grind I could not reciprocate. I remember high top
fades and peace signs cut into my gumby doo. I remember thinking I
was a militant cause I sported Afro medallions and had discovered
Marley and Malcom X. I remember starting to like being a blakkboy. I
remember starting to like Black boys.

Somewhere here in this present I am letting melancholia lure my mind
back to blues-filled front porches and hallelujah church deacons at the
local missionary Baptist down the road. I am remembering the sweet
cut of locker-room funk and conversations about how good some girl
can kiss or 'bout what nigga shot another last week. I am remembering
hot b-ball practice and sweat drops at line drills and worryin' if my
mama was at home with the little ones and daddy showed up again. .
.drunk or just mad. I am recalling unrequited, unexpressed romances
and escapisms. I am letting the dust from that dirt road that is now
pave. . . settle. And I am being guided to an endless road that you walk
until the mutt or Baby Sis or Uncle Webster come lookin' for ya.
Somewhere back there is myself: tucked away under a rock, tadpoling
down a creek, landing on a pondleaf, a happy day-old butterfly.

coming to rhyting

I knew the word was mighty. The words got stuck in the throat and started to bleed out of my pen-tip. Lonely and searching for some sign of myself near a red-dirt clay clearing at the edge of a piss-pond, I took notice of an old tree hanging onto its last green limb, a tadpole pushing herself through the masses for sustenance, and a slow-ass caterpillar with his Mississippi humpback soul train ascend up a leaf like, "I'm beautiful damnit!" Abstract and cynical, I began to imagine myself master of these things, master of the mighty word. Ebonic configurations meshed with missionary Baptist incantations and a harmonica wail. "The most beautifullest things in this world is just like that"[2]: simple, queer, spirit-filled, rhythmic, courageous, full of potential.

Not all things were beautiful. I had to find the courage to write of patrilineal madness, maternal secrets, and the burden of a biblical name. And I had to find the rhythm to recognize my beat: some deep house, reggae blend with hip-hoptic melodies. I had to be spirit-filled enough to let my hands dance on the page like a pick-a-ninny catching the spirit. And I had to be queer enough to embrace the complexities of an intersected identity. I had to be brave enough to write about desire for same and not opposite. There was hunger and it deepened the poverty of my desire: unrequited, unnamed, shamed. So I had to come to terms with the fact that the place where I shit wasn't a running toilet; and that I had to walk ath-a-letic bare feet back to the back of outhouses to sense my stink.

But I recognized that the privileged shit stank too; and the straight folks' too. 'Cause what's more common than our blood than our doo doo? Writing became that process whereby I ingest the magic and madness around me and dropped shit. On occasion, still, the nature around me asks: Feel that lyric? Can you smell it?

I knew the word was mighty when I knew I was the shit.

---

2 *The Most Beautifullest Thing in This World* is the debut studio album from American hip hop artist Keith Murray, released November 8, 1994 on Jive Records.

negation

if my father knew
the seed that he planted
was the one which would become
his second son
I am certain that he would have
spilled it on the ground
stepped on it and spit on it
and said:
"I WILL NOT HAVE A FAGGOT SON"
"WHAT AN ABOMINATION"
and felt proud.

I am sure that he would not realize
all of the beauty
and growth, and potential, and joy
his seed might bring
to the world.

I wonder why I still love that man so?
perhaps it is because
through his negation of me
I've discovered the greatest love of all;
and by observing him
I've learned not to take
too much shit offa' anyone,
and to be too proud, too black,
and too strong.

Thank you papa!

ten
(a rap)

age ten/ 5th grade crush on a twin named Tracy/ she lived on some suburban block/ on the better side of town in Little Rock/ nice girl...once mailed her a letter/ even though everyday at lunch and re- cess we made it a point to be together/ age ten heartbreak/ I remember it clear as day/ no schoolyard warning 'bout corrections/ red pen marks on my heart: the letter confessin' affections/ grammar check guised as class inspection rejection/ no longer second guessin' if I was her elec- tion/ guess I was not her kind of nigga/ least her moms and pops didn't think so/ they see no ghetto negro projection of higher plateaus/ wished I was bourgie but not on 1320 Monroe/ where the only pop music was th' big shots, th' glocks, and th' po po/

age ten/ negotiating nerdism with hangin' with thug friends/ every now and then couldn't win/ fighting demons within/ grapplin' with some Judeo Christian scare tactics: s.i.n. sin I'm in at age ten/ vomiting shame in trash bins/ two mile hikes down to Safeway on 12th Street/ food stamp shame for tryin' to eat/ non-st st st stuttered speech/ blakkboy: these were the ugly years though no oxycutum pimples/ just pre-junior high hygienics, kinda simple/ not yet a sex symbol/ cause ya broke and tryin' not to get choked on the second bowl of oatmeal, Malt-o-Meal, glad to have a meal meal, Tang with government cheese meal sammich meal deal, ya feel?/ age ten was real real.

body talk
(for "cool papa": a changing man)

her body   my body   his body
and then
his body   all over   her body

his fist strike blows to the face
that smiles to me at night
and chases away goblins
and stir grits that provide
more than   mere sustenance.
the cyclic spinning of her spoon
parallels the revolution
in her womb
that gave birth to me
who is bearing witness to see

her body   my body   his body
and then
his body   all over   her body.

he is not always violent.
sometimes I think that he is more
handsome than cruel,
but more often a punk:
shouting when he should cry
crushing and sucker-punching his vulnerability
out on mama's mouth;
telling me foul-ass and
contradictory things like
"always protect your mama. . .
even against me". . . said he
as if he couldn't help himself
or restrain blows or choking hands.

me. . . doing what his body say do
some days place   my body
between his   and her body—
my mama's body
tired of it
and no longer mustering the breath
nor the fight to scream   anymore.

me. . . once took a cut from the blade
intended for her
that didn't go deep at all
but forever impressed itself
underneath my skin.
did just what daddy told.
my body protecting her body   against his.

growing up
not wanting to be like him
like his body
I contemplated the opposite of hitting
the opposite of him
identification with the side of the man
dad was most afraid of
the side that was handsome
that hugged me good-n-stuff,
and that picked me out an afro
just like his.

yeah. . . daddy's little boy.
a mama's boy
trying to write words that resolve
those living and breathing memories.
trying to love all our bodies—
crying in order to erase
horror-wounds with
soft-blue pen tears
years later.
wanting a body-talk medicine
that cures remembering
of its trauma.

wanna make me   a better body
than his body
a better body
a my body   body   anybody
can body-love.

Freestyle Bored: Country Gramma

seldom floored by this freestyle
bored from the humdrum of abstract cats
bein' pimped for lyrical contracts
my poetix be Deleuzian
Negritude the paradigm shift,
(re)focus so as not to confuse them
ZEN imagery manifest synonyms:
choose him AND choose a life of sin?
compulsory. knew no better then
beat self up. sharp box cuts, b-boy bluffs
made me wanna fuck some niggas up
Easy E. crooned meditation hymns
tongue flick bottom lip, grip the dick
learn performative gestures: face cringe
rhytes of passage to manhood
moved while my shadow stood still
was that really keepin' it real?

hard handed back slaps from punk ass men
underestimate a phagg's thick skin
scary hard core tactics never scare me
my breath invests a thousand night-sweats
HIV drugs more threatenin' to me
I be 25 times 4, one breath for each season
Winter Spring Summer Fall-O my rhyme or reason.
bodies without organs play soft
malleable beat-box manifest in coughs
crucifix kiss innocence lost.
my naive native tongue is high strung
scans deep dictionaries for libido lexicons
words ebonically transformed
and mariposas swarm 'til dusk turns to dawn.

flow from West to East
washed out dirty tongues released.
my rhytes date back to 1986 bunkbeds
baby brotha chest pains, first cum stains
first self-cipher
inauguration to the rap game

it was me rappin' against three "eyes"
the self "eye" didn't like
wounded the me "eye" couldn't see
leavin' the third "eye" lonely?
Pulpit spit still scolds me!
learned to love my third eye outta shame
country mutt barked "you dope" as refrain
lost myself, it's a new game
no concrete just red dirt road
harmonizin' with toad croaks
crickets spit night beatz to spark lyrical fits.
as 25 I use'ta rhyme in my sleep
when city ciphers use'ta sleep on me
country gramma rooted deep as Oak trees.
Rhytes deferred 'til D.E.N in '92
mirrors began to reflect an "eye"
who said I love you: killed the other two
formed a coup with straight cats:
sport Duke blue
Southern crunk boy freestylin' miles away
with urban warriors now happy and gay
abstraction's just a fraction
my cerebral archive's never slackin'

my spinal taps nostalgia
to engage my "see" drive
third eye overrides the diss-guys
I'm Twenty Five

niggapoem
(for lil' blackboys in Lower Arkansas)

nigga nigga nigga
some figga we would no longer be that
if we erased letters from texts
eliminate "i", "g", "n", "e", "r"
from the alphabet.
some feel that it would hurt less
if the sound betrayed and alienated
the tongues of bigots.
but that can't be...
and I don't want no part
in that PC fiction.

as a child
the air never swallowed up
the hate of such injurious word-thangs,
nor their history.
so erased from texts
or censored in speech
"nigger" would mock us still
in the white imagination.
(when he see or follow me
what do he see?)
"NIGGER!"
sometime without saying a word.

so I refuse to give them credit
for their word.
nor do I want to dismiss
what grandma spoke 'bout
sticks and stones.
she say: "if it mean ignorant,
then that ain't me anyway."
and jumping to cut with my fists
might only verify that I understand
white definitions
as my blakk truth.

nigga nigga nigga nigga nigga
repeated enough
becomes nothing but an utterance.

and if "words will never hurt me"
then why the hell should a sound?

so me and friends
and brothas and sistas
improvise that sound-thang like jazz.
we replace their "er" with our "a"
"nigger" ebonically transfigured
becomes "nigga"
'cause we make it not-the-same.
and these days
I refer to the man I most love
as my nigga.
we exchange love and understanding
through that sound
of pain and history we sense
like river deep—
a psychic inversion
that strips the word of hate,
rendering it loving.
and sometime it even warrant a smile.
that word...
it don't hurt no more... it heals.
now I know:
that "n" word, the definition
no white man owns
any more than I.

weakened nights

five out of the seven nights
breathing is easier
and on the labored nights I recall
some crazy tale, I was told by a Cherokee ancestor.
she often visited me
when I was losing myself in the thick of self-loathing
and came to cool the air, wipe sweatbeads
and do crazy-ass, disruptive riddles.

once she said
falling stars are caught
by subtle and lonely green pastures.
that they welcome the caress of the explosion
that they tuck the stars inside they mud
for safekeeping and hard times.
she said this method
recognized only by rain-gods
makes the ground fertile.
while earthmen
see only damage and ruin
if anything at all.

I didn't understand her nonsense
not then;
but some years later
I began to let myself love again.
and I understood.

five out of the seven nights
breathing is easier.
there are traces of his presence
from the: "goodnight" or "I miss you."
they are soundwaves that pierce the stars;
they is heaven-lights that laugh and blush
as if to mock my reaction to his soul-speak.
me and him are many miles apart
but them there stars relish our puppy love
innocent and unconstrained
nonetheless true.

'cause on the other two nights
that are volatile and less secure
the stars seem to betray the night sky—
their confident glow sneak away,
like my own,
and I sometime give into
past insecurities and 3 a.m. whereabouts
contemplating who warms him
besides me.

on these most endless nights
there are fewer reminders
that I am liked a whole lot too.

to remember that I am thought of:
there are two-day-old phone-tag
or "I-just-called-to-say" messages,
there are concentrations on his photo-frame,
and prayers at a shrine I've built that
obliterates the empty.

and in the dark
I transfigure the pillows beneath me.
I make them a heartbeat,
and the corners of their cushion-frame,
hands that hold and fold into my own.
And when I kiss the fluff of their neck
I make-believe that I am tasting the musk of his.

my spirit ancestor would validate
these imaginings.
she'd say:
"You not crazy...
just crazy about him.
That's what green earth do.
How else to catch a falling star?"

Diss Course

my voice is trapped inside of
cultural discourse
eclipsing my ebonics
so my spirit is wailin'
to reconcile itself with electronic
technocratic madness and magic
and I've become an addict,
a postmodern neither-nor,
a little boy's secret toy,
a personified metaphor,
a simple symbol,
a jazz suite,   a skipped heartbeat
the ironic nasty unique stink
of clorox bleach.

Cultural discourse is a plain mess
made jargonesque.
My guess is that next
they'll be new words, new worlds,
subject verb disagreements,
dull adverbs that don't mean shit.

I want the cultural discourse of
my naive native tongue
wrenching from the gut of burial grounds
drooling out the mouths of crack babies,
creaking out of mesh-net
Southern fried front porches
who got they own cultural discourses
simple as silence.

There,
where nappy loud people laugh
and fondle they lovers,
there is an exotic hula dancer blackgirl,
a gran Aunties eye roll back at'cha,
a baby's hunger screaming
inside of her ashy tears.

Discourse be
the necessity of a Sunday dinner ham-hoc
signifying more than history or anthropology,
more than lineage or genealogy.

My grammatology speaks trip-hop blues
verbal tools abused and misused,
gettin' mistaken
for the simplicity of bacon smells
and well water.
I wanna holler, laugh out loud
rebuke cultural discourses.

I think I better let go of Foucault
and discipline my nose and lil' ears
to hear the theory of Uncle Bam's madness
the song of Sheniqua's smile,
the rhythm of Tay Tay's heartbeat.
My beginnings start with the thick of cum stains
my frame of skeleton and shame is
anti-cultural diss course
is spoken by disenfranchised chilren
who speak *boricua* and nigga and *patois*
it is their hick-ups, their whispers,
their steady
          steady
                    dreams.

Breath 2

Soul Searchin'

National Blakk Anthem
(for Washington and Grandpa Hillard)

My country 'tis of thee
there are lil' blakkboys
who will never see the sunset *there*
but who understand their blue-black skin
within which heart beats   just-the-same
steady   steady
keepin'em goin' when
their silent stares get misread
as defiance   or rebellious   or ignorant niggerish craze
when their smiling too much
is read as cunning or lazy or remedial
or their not smiling enough
as bestial or delinquent or criminal
by a people who analyze even their waking.

heart beat persist like hypnotic
beating of drums
black feet steady dancing on fertile ground
happy smiles and screams and wails
that are smarter and more sensible
than any discourse the colonizer say
will make us more civilized
without telling or informing us
that civilization's bad side is that
we will most certainly be less alive
than our blue-black African movements.
they fail to mention that the uprooting and violence
civilization requires
might make us forget that we had our own
before theirs
forget also
our origins   and think we sprung up
in cotton fields
somewhere down dirty South.

there are lil' blakkgirls
recognizing something called
différance, alterity, otherness,
and internalizing the shame/self-loathing
that was never theirs

lil' blakkgirls sometimes vomit it back out
realizing that it was prank-poison wrapped
pretty pink.
if not she blakk and misrecognizing
her blue-black kin
across waters in
Senegal, Brazil, U.K, Haiti, Costa Rica, Bordeaux,
or Eastside or Westside or other part of town
browns
as foreigner-enemies
without questioning the allegiance and patriotism
she has borrowed from a people
who bruised and traumatized
kinky headed little blakk girls
not light years before.

Som'ma us didn't always know bout
the Africa in our dance and hum and music
and art and soul and sensibility and struggle.
We were lil' pickaninnies screaming bout'
Michael Jackson "Thriller"
and moonwalking
though convinced at school
that we could never be astronauts.
And when they showed us "Roots" on TV
we went back to the schools
shocked and terrified and felt-lied-to
and ourselves whipped and carrying
Kunta Kinte scars   back
to third grade discussions 'bout
the great Columbus and Shakespeare
and Napoleon.

They failed to tell us
there are others ways we be blakk
and OK to want to be,
and that our happy dancing rhythmic feet
come from some place
that is more than the hunger and war
we see of the Africa on TV.

we
having stupidly repeated hateful phraseology
like African booty
scratching for ways to place the guilt
somewhere else.
we were sometimes never told the story
but knew it wasn't such a great idea
to be too blakk in the world.

But some blakkboys and blakkgirls
made pacts to themselves
and each other
to love they black self
and love those whose black silence
is sometimes the only peace-talk
they can manage to dream-up.
and yes we said
when we get real-bigger
that we would absorb pages
through the pores and wounds
that celebrate the places we come from
that some of us will never see
except through looking at each other
or freeing ourselves enough to dream.

we would learn the other side of blakkness
that is still black African
and would not buy into the
conquer and divide
"they ain't you cause they speak
different languages and got different
grades of hair or melanin
or serve different gods."

We
blakkboys and blakkgirls would make a
telepathic transnational pact
with brothers and sisters 'round the world
to remember that our silences
and our movement and our pain
has common origins all the same.

blue-blakk revolutionaries
whose remembering and self-love
feet-stomping, spirit-filled, body
reverberations
and gyrations and frustration
and scientific, mathematical brilliance
philosophical mind-boggle
and tolerance and compromise

might someday
shake the world
into something better
that we are proud to love
cuz it is our hard earned
fought for
freedom.

Magnetix[3]
(for dad and joseph)

I have loved black men
agitated by the thick of it…
guarded like when they anticipate
the sting of a racial slur,
or a gender reprimand
for not being a manly enough boy.
I have caressed the tight in their backs
still longing for fathers to come back
with explanations for absence.

I have encountered baby daddies
oblivious to the souls that haunt them daily
in order to stay sane—
Mandingo sons, weakened by their own
sense of potentiality
and too many deferred dreams.

I have forgiven men who have
inherited cycles that return
deadly as a boomerang.
I have kissed them
before they could speak sharp words,
like what they silence say.
I have held their hand for dear life
before they could strike me
with they fists,
or pull a gat on me
for reflecting they black back to them:
beautiful
in ways that would bring them to tears
if they accepted it.

And I have been a man
terrified of being loved by these men,
preferring lonely corners or playboy paraphernalia
to being cradled
and feeling safe enough to cry.

---

3 "Magnetix" was also published in the anthology *Freedom In This Village: Twenty-Five Years of Black Gay Men's Writing*, edited with an introduction by E. Lynn Harris (Carrol & Graf publishers, 2005).

I have been a man
who has witnessed my brother fall
just as his fingertips admit vulnerability
outstretched and longing for connection
and falling
like rainbows
foreshadow a smile.

I have been a man
who smiles when I want most
not to
show
that side of myself—
trusting and delighted
like a lil nappyheadedblakkboy
unafraid of afro picks,
or being found hiding
by another blakk boy
behind a lil' tree
half my size.

I have been a reflection of myself
in the morning,
eyes blushing or troubled or smiling
and wondering
what kind of man I will be
today, tomorrow
And shedding yesterday's illusion of failure
for a better man
standing strong
open to loving, real good,
especially
          myself.

wrong hood

hot as hell up in this piece
please do not mistake my sweat for tears
nor my daunting gaze
for anger.

it's nice and sunny and lite
outside   in Palo Alto
and two days ago
some cracker yelled at me: "BOY!"
(I guess I didn't supposed to be in his hood).

the birds even
echo that damn word: "BOY!"
they do not sing lite,
Palo Alto-like

do not mistake their song for
happy happy.
they probably pissed
just like me
not crying
just hot and a little uncomfortable,
sweating at the eyes.

Oakland

I need my blackness close to me.
Snug tight like grandmama's quilt on a chilly mid-morning.
Black like the sediment when you smell it.
Black like the safety of quiet under eyelids
        during some beautiful daydream.
or like the graying blakklady dreadlock goddess
        glance at you on BART
cuz whitefolk's kids are acting "typical"
and you are both grinding your teeth
underneath a polite smile, like:
        "they so cute!"
when you know they bad asses
and kicking the back of your seat
        and you tryin' to sleep!
Real black like you or her gonna get if they don't quit.

Like the lack of it you sense
across the bridge   in that city with the black mayor
but fewer   and fewer   and fewer black people.
Black like our mayor here ain't.

I need my blackness close to me.
Smug like the sunny smile I get from some
        headwrapped sistah stridin' round the lake.
Black like the undercurl of my napps.
Like the rhythmic way we speak and gesture and laugh.

I need my blackness close to me.
Like mirrors reflecting my black back to me
        or the depth of my baritone poem.
Like history ain't in public schools.
Black like the infinite universe
        or like black art that has that scent and shine.

And like the ghetto girlz on the corner
that make your eyes roll back and tummy tight
        cuz they look a mess and they babies look worse
        but they your peoples anyway
        and this is Oakland
        and the way you like it:
Snug   Tight   Black.

Soul Unfinished

Soul is unfinished
if you listen deep enough
in the cavity of your own medulla oblong
gotta stand in front of a mirror to check the fog
of your breath
to witness this soul shape.
for when the breath goes
so goes the soul.

funny how some use mirrors
to check how tight they flesh is
round the eyes
or if the hair is falling or kinking
dredlocking or Afro-puffing right.

funny how some use mirrors
to check if they body look more like a
line, a circle, rectangle, or hourglass
when no amount of Slim Fast or soul food can
redeem the spirit.

funny how they checking
shell pulled on top of the shell
of skin and bones and muscle.
Check the breath at mirrors
when the breath goes
so goes you.

don't think for a minute that
collard greens and sweet potato pie
can heal soul wounds.
But hear a black lady croon a blues
on a front porch
and you'll   feel   soul
tingling the fingertips and joints.
styling a freestyle pose
iterating a point.

so, what is soul?
Soul is some body and me making kinetic energy
under bedroom sheets.

Soul is so pretty it dances circles
contorts itself into liquids
like tears and sweat
and the musky stank after b-ball
sessions in West Oakland.

funk is soul expressin' itself
free from rationality and logic
Soul don't always make sense
don't care about being adorned
with dollars and cents
each soul has its own scent.

watch a little youngster or a puppy yawn:
Soul is the flex of body stirring the
stretch of the back and arms
up and around
pop locking, eyes bulging
ghetto girl   arms raising:
"hey . . . that's my song . . .
I'm just Mary Mary"
and everybody is just Merry Merry
when they got soul.

Soul like
that B-boy bouncing his headphoned head
to some beat eyes closed
Soul is in church and in blakk music.
gospel music that is
weighty with DeAngelo crooning.
Soul is spirit looming over the funeral box
the sum/total of sorrow megadeath
gliding over the Afro-American cemetery
the virtual ghettos
keeping the skeleton bones
Middle passage-tight and next to each other
cause blakk people forgot to speak to each other
in passing.

I found soul dancing
in a Bedstuy cipher one day:
Hancock and Nostrand

winter-rhymes
pushing circles out shaping
a revolutionary army.

I watched the soul circles breath made
cause the bruh was rhyming bout bitches,
bitch niggas, and faggots
so he didn't know his soul
though I took the time to see it.

the depth of the wail is spiritual
the "umph" unspoken but felt after the "o my lord...."
the burst of light beckoned by an unsuspecting melody.
Harmonies connect soul   so soul is that
Soul is blakk.
Soul is white boy or girl
unafraid to step into they blakkness.
it is Latino or Asian tasting the thick of they blakk.
Soul is Native.
Soul is Aretha bringing church to the juke joint.
Soul is James gettin' the spirit   fallen
and resurrected by church deacons.

Soul is the reverberation of the unspoken
a rhythm-rhyme that betrays the mimic.
What is soul?

you cannot perceive it
except to swallow the very depths of
cemetery dirt
full of bones and skeletons
awaiting a dance with you, the living
wanting a taste of your breath
to remind them that their terror and struggle
and pain were not in vain.

I got soul . . . 'cause I know   my breath
well   enough
to just   be   with it.
And quit trying to explain
What soul is
    when it   just
is.

Flight 4494

niggas got no business in
little White Plains
engulfed in big white fluff
had enough of that stuff
on ground
where I'm broke and queer
and brown

and it ain't that I ain't tough enough
to brave that stuff
'cause up here or down there
the air is mighty rough

I'm just trying to save my strength
for when I'm down.

the opposite of me . . . rhyting

the opposite of me
rhyting
is my silence
or my song.
my saying nothing is
just as powerful   as words
'specially   when rhyting is war by
other means
and fighting   needless virility.

I would rather scribble sounds
that unwrite blood battles
and that disarm old his/stories
of verbal weaponry and
vio lent   enlighten   ment
and instead
take pleasure in the pandemonium
of blank-like and savage
blakk pages
and still-life rhythms
I let be
just that   when I be
unwilling to participate in reasoning
sometime   and
just wanna celebrate
this Africa-thang that has never
talked more beautiful—
a de-inking, metaphysical erasure
capable of putting colonizing
words that throat-cut
on pause.

so if by rhyting on the silence
of pages
with innocent alphabets
scrambled in order
          to inscribe winners
and losers—

or the page-lines even
that dissect and prevent the merging of
the said and
not   yet   said

        if by following these conventions
I prevent myself from imagining
what might be
(a momentary site void of struggle?)
then being open to infinite possibilities,
a beauty unrepresentable by words
unseen and unwitnessible
by grammatical and syntactical eyes
becomes the sweetest
and most desperate maneuver
I can sing.

in between gunfire
during the safer dreams of a
black/white nothingness,
there is a story that is
the opposite of me
that I make myself tell myself
in order to have a peace-moment.
not a silence that is absence.
sometime
        it speaks in moans   grunts
hums   and   o'lauwdies
wails falsetto or blues-like
for the pain
written as words
is never enough.

Picture This

Mumia was framed
A black border
pretty-like   circumscription
in rectangular shape.
His emotion and experience
captured into pictures
that translate the moment
into romance
due to demands by supporters
with conditions
requiring
that he look rebel enough
to fight for
and his face made symbol
and story forgotten.

Yeah
Mumia was framed.
His name made eponymous with
the insane system
and uttered repetitiously as refrain
until famed enough
to put on signs at concerts.

And well-intentioned progressives
prematurely make a martyr out of man
who ain't dead   yet
and who they trying to keep alive
seeing no contradiction.

Mumia was framed
Double double by them and we.
Now
looking at him pictured
me,
wanting to take for a smile
what may have been a grimace
moments earlier.
We know   photos
lie like police investigators
and their lie detectors.

His frame-face plastered all over
looking pleasant enough
to be read as nice-like
or an eccentric friend—
an articulate enough blakk
can make his plea believable.

They framed Mumia.
Sho did.
And Others
should be sign posts
too
made interchangeable stories
represented by
more than
just one
frame.

The Others
dread   locked   up
Brothas without the journalism
and charisma,
the popularity or support
to rhyte resistance behind bars.

Pro-Lifer

(Tick tock   tick tock)
Metaphors don't come so sweet these days
'cause niggaboys and girls
are pronounced dead at birth
the killing deferred
      (Tick tock   tick tock)
by a system that hides
behind lies and fabricates truths and
creates criminals and crack addicts
and hookers.

System sends agents down
      (Tick tock   tick tock)
to temper and seduce and quell
revolutionaries with
cars and clothes and jewels and Benjamins
What?!
What but the kindness and benevolence
Of tricksters
the last supper
before the
      (Tick tock   tick tock)
Death wish
Before the execution

Picture that:
an organized, convenient unrest/protest
Where lines are comfortably drawn
And "them" don't look like "us"
And there is time
to plan our anger out
And we are really
Really   really
Ready to die
      (Tick tock   tick tock)
before they come to get us.

Me   starting to question why
I   am
one of ten blakk bodies
at a two-hundred people rally

(Tick tock   tick tock)
"Where my niggas is at? Where my niggas is at?"
"Where my ladies is at? Where is my ladies is at?"
(Tick tock   tick tock)
Perhaps niggas are too busy shooting
up
and killing each other
and entering Jerry Springer sweepstakes
and running for political offices
and running to the beach
to get more sand
for the hourglass
(Tick tock   tick tock)
not infinite
just managed by the choices we make
or choose not to—
how fast we run or whether or not we wear
the right Nikes
or drink Sprite at half-time.

Perhaps niggas like me should be
pondering the picture of lil' brother
locked down at Tucker Max
for somebody's convenience who
don't even know his name.
There ain't rallies for him
except for the crying at my altar.
What do we make of the nameless hundreds?
Wait
'til it get more desperate
the hours before execution
before we respond/react.

Looking around at the rally
I see three brothas
two are cops waiting for me to
breathe insurrection too loudly.
The other is a dis/eased homeless man
with nothing to lose
but his lonely night-shadow
and the scent he no longer senses
'cause makes no cents.
(Tick tock   tick tock)

I looked for Assata there
for inspiration
but she ain't allowed Westside
Stateside or any side   here.
And it again occurred to me
that niggababies are
pronounced dead at birth
in Amerika
placed on the waiting list
and in the mean time
playing musical chairs
for the
you got the right one baby
chair
with straps and lil' hat and
Lectricity   E   lectricity.

There are holding pens
for revolutionaries
who never got the chance to
plot and scheme against injustice
just chances to implicate themselves
in the conspiracies
          (*Tick tock   tick tock)*
Apocalyptic paranoia
          (*Tick tock   tick tock)*
Solitary confinement
          (*Tick tock   tick tock)*
Getting tired of getting tired
          (*Tick tock   tick tock)*
This shit is   serious
Niggababies are pronounced dead at birth
In Amerika
kill each other off
or sometimes
are
convicted for answering "no"
to the question: "did you kill?"
without being informed
the question would be changed to

"Did you not?"
and the reply "no"
kept.
>   *(Tick tock   tick tock)*

"Don't push me
'cause I'm close to the

>   Edge."

And these marches and protests
are wearing on my spirit
>   *(Tick tock   tick tock)*
One nigga of ten at the rally
trying to assert my presence
in the absence of
Niggababies
growing and grown.
Me
deferring the deferral
the pronouncement of my death
made years ago
>   *(Tick tock   tick tock)*
deferring death
for just one more
>   *(Tick tock   tick tock)*
one more
>   Tick tock.

Gaze on Mandingo, an Introduction

"Black Men Loving Black Men Is *The* Revolutionary Act"
                                    —Marlon Riggs, *Tongues Untied*

"It is necessary to grow a new skin, to develop new thoughts, to set afoot a new man"
                                    —Frantz Fanon

"Diamonds are coals under pressure"
                                    —Nina Simone

As a young male growing up in several U.S. ghettos (both urban and rural), I was aware of the multiple implications of being black. I came to know that being a black male meant being subjected to a whole host of incompatible representations. As if it was not enough to be subjugated by white racism, there were the judgments made by other blacks or the reproach of my own self-reflexive gaze. Ambitious, project-boy... not like the others, not hardly a delinquent (not yet), promising, but a little hostile...yeah. There were, in addition, prescriptions for what kind of black man I should become: a tough, intelligent, well assimilated, and still-down-with-my-people, streetsmart man. Unsurprisingly, I struggled with how to uncover a sense of self from all the expectations. The images of black men made available through the media and television were either hypermasculine superheros in Blaxploitation flicks or frustrated "boyz in the hood" whose rage with societal racism frequently got played out in multiple, self-destructive reactions. I tried to counter these images with a paradoxical performance of ghettoman savvy: black enough and man enough to substantiate that I was "down" with the brothas, yet articulate and poised enough to maneuver my way through the complex maze of white sociality and privilege.

There were moments when I thought that I would lose myself in whiteness; but I believed strongly that acting like a good *boy* would save me from the racist presuppositions that seemed most inescapable. I figured that I could charm "The Man"—a near-omnipotent whiteness that was too disparate and subtle to locate but that was always working to subjugate. I naively believed that self-alignment could be a sure way out of the realities of race and believed that if my performance was shrewd enough, I might be granted some room to breathe— perhaps even a space to create. This mediating space was, no doubt, a difficult place to be. I was embittered about this tense place in the middle that demanded constant negotiation: between Africa and America, home and the academy, between a self that I thought I knew and the one I was trying to find. I was searching for a social space void of contradictions; and did not yet realize that no such place existed.

In college, my resistance took the form of a shaky appropriation of Afro-centric epistemology and a nostalgic appreciation for Black Power. I was trying to undo all the acculturation and find a (my)self that did not even exist. I had no idea then that finding oneself is an inherently contradictory process. Either we presuppose a self to be found (which altogether negates the need for a search) or we have no sense of what that self would resemble and, as such, are unable to recognize it when it comes into being. The search for self makes an enticing but deceptive promise; and I would later realize that searching for me was a much less productive process than becoming me.

A graduate student, my current intellectual projects scrutinize systems of domination that would have black men believe that the only identities available are the ones "The Man" prescribes. "Gaze On Mandingo"[4] is not just about my scrutinizing gaze on the black male bodies in James Mason's 1975 film "Mandingo." It is not just about exercising a critical gaze on writings by black intellectuals who attempt to represent black masculinity; nor am I just interested in confessing my own voyeuristic and ethnographic gaze on contemporary "Mandingo"-men. The question that centrally informs this work is how black men might turn the gaze on ourselves—initiate acts of self-reflexivity that can give rise to alliances that resist the sources of our subjection? Might self-introspection be a neglected site of subversion that can propel collective resistance against the sources of our subjection? I am interested in generating a discussion about how ethical experience can be shaped in ways that affect the political, economic, and social structures that subjugate us. I am interested in "flipping the script"—in challenging the ways that black men internalize identities that we ourselves took no part in creating. I am specifically concerned about the ways that socially constituted antagonisms between black men hinder politically effective coalitions and want to interrogate this outgrowth of internalized oppression and its consequences. I am most

---

4 Mandingo are a people geographically located in the upper Niger valley in West Africa. Many people do not know this, as what the catchword signifies for many Americans is the colloquial and sexualized appropriation of the term that emerges in the popular Blaxploitation film, "Mandingo"—a movie based on the 1957 novel by Kyle Onstott. Mandingo has come to represent the toughness, virility, and sexual prowess of black men. Sadly, an internet search is likely to produce more websites about how to enhance male sexual prowess than anything about Africa.

troubled when I see the ways that the black male scripts we perform are complicit with our own domination.

For many black men, the Million Man March provided one such opportunity to reinvigorate a political struggle that would address American racism and its multiple effects. Black men gathered to acknowledge the ways in which our conduct is often in accord with the distressing predicaments and negative indicators within our community. Imperative political transformations would not occur without black men undertaking a personal introspective process directed towards self-evaluation and personal development. For some of us, the March was about launching personal interventions, teasing out complexities, owning our fabrications and performances, and reconstructing black male experience in order to transform ourselves and the communities in which we live. I found some hopefulness in the possibility that black men were interested in engaging in a self-fashioning that reminded me of the ethical experience Michel Foucault celebrates in the latter volumes of *History of Sexuality*. I especially thought about his belief that the "work of the self on the self" can become indispensable to understanding (and engaging in) political struggle. Directing political acts that are grounded in ethical reflection seems a more productive strategy than either hoping for some divine rescue or organizing anti-hero militias with no real objectives beyond destroying "The Man." "The Man," like the subjectifying power "he" personifies, is here to stay, even as "his" face is ever-changing.

October 16, 1995, was a day that, for me, marked the possibility for collectively reconceptualizing black male experience. Because it was principally a day about possibilities, I was ambivalent about precisely what kind of re-conceptualization would take place. I feared that any national conversation about black manhood could potentially promote some icon of black manhood that negates much of what I am: black and male certainly, but a good deal more as well. As a gay brotha who is largely inspired by my studies of feminism, I feared that mobilizing American black men would lead to essentializing, one-dimensional conceptions of manhood that reinforce and mirror the white heteronormative standards I have struggled against since childhood. White patriarchy in blackface can hardly characterize political subversion; it can only reinforce the current order.

My reservations about attending the Million Man March were connected with the race-essentializing, patriarchal and heterosexist ideology so subtly central to much of its inception. Like many others I would cling to the more general call for personal introspection: the kind of self-evaluation that I believe is so central to building self-confidence, promoting self-determination, and actualizing political transformation. An optimist, I hoped that this mobilization would be the impetus for the creation of strong coalitions upon which political struggles can depend. Black men would collectively raise thoughtful challenges to institutional racism as well as social and economic injustice. Men markedly different than me would recognize that despite our differences, we share common concerns. The March would be a forum where black men could address our (often) antagonistic relationships to each other and to the women and children in our lives. We might recognize the extent to which patriarchal models necessitate the very domination and subjugation we struggle against. It would be a day filled with both idealism and anxiety, the kind of apprehensive excitability common to all great moments in history.

My hope was that the Million Man March could encourage a recognition of all the things that had been preventing meaningful and politically effective coalitions among black men. The question of exactly what we as black men would fight for, what we would change, is a complex and sophisticated question that I could not expect the March to answer. However, I believed that this collective mobilization was, itself, revolutionary. If only temporarily, there was a moment in America's history where black men were really about loving each other: petty prejudices were deferred, narrow political and religious ideologies were (often) made secondary to common goals, physical expressions of same gender love in the form of hugs and kisses were sanctioned, tears did not signify the "punk," but rather, a new kind of brotha on that day. It was a moment that foreshadowed true personal subversions and that represented revolutionary possibilities. I would reconcile my differences with the March organizers by recognizing that my participation was itself a struggle that would provide its own meaningful lesson: the realization that there is no singular model for black men and that our collective strength lies in our diversity.

A few years after the march and having developed a strong desire to grapple intellectually with the complex nature of black male experience, I have located academia as a place where I can think productively about systems of subjectification, the relation between power and the subject, ethical self-formation and political agency. From this vantage point, there seemed to be a lack of clarity about what March leaders' call for atonement was asking of us. In one sense, atoning involves self-critique. Black men *should* think about what within us is lacking, about dreams deferred, about talents we have not ourselves recognized amid all the preoccupation with scrutiny from the whites, from black women, from each other.

For many black men, the process of atonement encouraged by the Million Man March culminated with self-assessment. Expiating or reconciling one's failures should have been (in more cases than I have seen since the March) an impetus for instituting personal and institutional changes beyond the repentant act. Atonement in this partial sense is problematic if it calls upon black men to locate problems and acknowledge faults, but is conceptualized in such a way that men perpetually make amends for failures and attempt to undo wrongs without a strategy for building something positive. Black men become atoning animals—seeking redemption *ad infinitum.* While atonement as the recognition of a problem can be productive in the sense that it calls for self-evaluation and redescription, it fails as long as it is more concerned with undoing and atoning than creating and becoming. Our subjugation and psychological scars are not things we can undo; neither are our mistakes and failures. As with the Deleuzean[5] fold, there is something fundamentally unproductive about the attempts to unfold. Once the crease is made, it makes little sense to keep pressing eternally in order to undo the (undoable) fold. Even a reversal of the fold is no more than a new fold—a return (or folding back) to the initial injury rather than an undoing of it. I believe that instead of struggling and pressing to erase our subjugation, black men should concern ourselves with (and focus our energies towards) the creative process of seizing the agency to make new folds. I am not advocating the kinds of stylistic folds that open up a space for creative expression (such as some forms of Hip-Hop music) but which devalue black life through promoting material excess and violence within our communities. Rather, I am proposing that black men produce folds that are always self-critical and that attempt to anticipate and eschew the forms of domination responsible for our subjugation.

---

5 As I understand Deleuze's essay "How Do You Make Yourself A Body Without Organs," the Body Without Organs describes a plane of consistency that resists organization (shaping) into a subjected organism. The fold signifies a moment of violence against the individual which cannot be undone. However, the BWO after subjectification is not rendered helpless: "We are continually stratified . . . The BWO is that glacial reality where the alluvions, sedimentations, coagulations, foldings, and recoilings that compose an organism—and also signification and subject—occur" (pg. 159). The "wrongfully folded" BWO might conceive of this folding as an opportunity for subversive agency. Deleuze says: "You have to keep enough of the organism for it to reform each dawn; and you have to keep small supplies of significance and subjectification, if only to turn them against their own systems when the circumstances demand it, when things, persons, even situations, force you to..." (pg. 160).

Perhaps the most disappointing aspects of the Million Man March were connected to its reduction to a single event. The inspiration and joy black men experienced at the event—even the delight that one produced by the mere reminiscence—would not be enough to actuate the kind of changes envisioned at the march. Sadly, for so many black men, remembering the March was about calling forth inspiration on difficult days in the predominantly white workplace or after being interrogated by the gaze of a suspecting salesperson. Looking for signs of brotherly love a year after the March, I became more frustrated than I had been before it. The mere anticipation of the event seemed to generate a vision that, afterwards, was suspended as many black men returned to business as usual.

A year following the March I was in Bedstuy,[6] daily reciprocating screwface gestures at brothas on the corner. Screwface is a gaze that scrutinizes the authenticity of another's manhood. It is a ritualistic practice that is so internalized and ingrained that the stroll around the corner store triggers an impulsive performance. I begin to contradict all those politically subversive stands that I relentlessly advocate in consciousness. The change in my pace marks the confrontation, the rhythm in my stride anticipates judgment, and I remove any visible signs of happiness (the last thing I want to do is to appear "gay"). So it is a habitual response to perform the mean-mug or screwface. Gnawing the teeth, perfectly reciprocating the daunting stares, a slight nod of the head and other small gestures constitute the complex game of reading the gaze:

> *Is this brotha tryin' to test me or size me up?*
> *Might it be all right to speak? If I look one se-*
> *cond too long at this brotha I might incite an*
> *unwanted confrontation. Damn he looks*
> *good! What was that look about? Oh shit, I*
> *forgot to hide my Foucault books. Look kinda*
> *silly frontin' like there is such a thing as a*
> *hard-core academician (an image that the*
> *brothas on this corner aren't likely to accept*
> *anytime soon).*

---

6 Bedstuy (Bedford-Stuyvesant) Brooklyn is one of the largest black communities in the United States. It was my neighborhood through the duration of my research at The Graduate Faculty at The New School for Social Research.

What is most problematic about this *round-the-way* ritual is not its performative nature. It is no more dramatic or exaggerated than the intellectual performance at the academic conference. In either situation I am capable of performing the gestures and jargon acceptably. I know what is expected of me and am familiar with the respective codes of conduct. So I am not writing about black men, masculine anxiety, and subjugation because I am interested in problematizing (inescapable) performances, but rather because I have serious concerns about mis-recognizing the ways certain of our performances are complicit with our own subjugation. That I can act—that I can consciously employ a subversive performance—opens up possibilities for understanding how performance can be exercised for survival and resistance. As I "Gaze On Mandingo," this idea of performative strategies of resistance is central to my examinations of black masculinity.

Resistance. What would it mean, for example, for me to deny the screwface performance on my Bedstuy streetcorner? What might he do if I extended my hand or initiated a brotherly embrace? Put a knife to my throat? Ask me out on a date? The possibilities are many; but the fear of antagonism is often enough to squelch attempts at bravery. Fear continues to operate as a mutual and reiterative function between black men. Too often, we are afraid to express love for each other. Let us show each other how afraid we are: (Screwface and head-nod: *"What up dawg?"* he says. *"Nothin, yo,"* I reply.) End scene.

> *So many roles for you to play*
> *just to stay in the game.*
> *Will you follow the lead*
> *or dance to the tune of a different beat?*
>
> *Mother, father, daughter or son,*
> *they're all one and the same.*
> *Then you discover you've played them so long*
> *you don't even know your name.*
>
> *After learning predetermined roles they set for you,*
> *now's the time to realize that you can do what you want to do.*[7]

I invoke the late Marlon Riggs' sentiment that "Black Men Loving Black Men Is The Revolutionary Act" because black men fighting and killing each other is the "business as usual" that I feared we would re-

---

7 Poem used in *Tongues Untied* by the late Marlon Riggs, adapted from song "Do What You Wanna Do" by Steven Langley.

vert to upon return from the Million Man March. Riggs recognized the danger that is connected with black men having to assume roles that lead to self-loathing. He wanted to call in question the lack of respect for brothas who are thinking creatively and critically about manhood. The very systems of power that work to subordinate black men are often the same systems that applaud our antagonism towards each other. If systems of domination can be personified as "The Man," then "he" is, no doubt, delighted when one black man dies by the hands of another. "He" understands black on black violence as a way that black men assist "him" in our own annihilation. Black on black violence simply makes "his" job easier. Black men have been conditioned to recognize the worthlessness we sometimes feel for ourselves in our mirror images—in each other. We repeatedly project our own self-loathing on those who most resemble us. Precisely who is the "bitch ass nigga" customarily referenced in so much of contemporary hip-hop? How do sexism and heterosexism inform this kind of scrutiny? Is this what the screwface signifies?

"To all the niggas and the hundred dollar billars, the real niggas that ain't got no feelings"[8]

What is a "real nigga" anyway, and how might we insist on its problematic valuation as a standard for black masculinity?

While I disagree that there is revolutionary potential that is particular to love between black men (romantic or otherwise) or that revolution should be reduced to the "act,"[9] I believe that it is precisely fear of love between brothas manifesting itself romantically (homophobia), that has long prevented love between black men which is not apologetic, defensive, or anxiety-ridden. Homophobia functions to rebuke what appears to be an extreme manifestation of love between men. Often, the capacity for one brotha to love another must be perpetually negated each time desire is felt. Getting beyond this fear, which I argue involves getting beyond black male homophobia, is a courageous process that is indeed revolutionary.

---

8 Lyrics to "Shook Ones" by Mobb Deep, on their album *The Infamous.*

9 Though Riggs' film *Tongues Untied* focuses on the self-determination of the black gay subject and celebrating romantic love and desire between black men, it does not follow that the "act" that he refers to when he suggests that "Black men loving black men is the revolutionary act," is necessarily a sexual one. I would caution against reducing revolution to any singular act, in the way that some counter-effective militant actions get labeled "revolutionary" based on the mere radical nature of the act.

Both W.E.B. DuBois and James Baldwin referred to a double-edgedness, a special sense, that comes from having to endure the process of subjugation. Can the injury performed by the violating other be reorganized in order to provide a strategic advantage—a counter-performance that transforms injury into insurgency? Might the physical and psychological scars dealt to black men give rise to what feminist Gloria Anzaldúa calls *la facultad*[10]—that special sensibility that those who are daily beaten-down rely on for survival? My belief is that if black men can begin to disavow unhappy attachments to our subjection, then we can begin the proactive process of becoming. Becoming expresses an optimistic and creative process that is not preoccupied with fighting off a subjection that we can never fully escape, but rather is about discovering ways to transform our subjection into a self-determined and politically viable existence.

Reflecting on my participation in the Million Man March, it is clear that the Million Man March will never represent the same thing for all black men. For me it will forever recall a moment when I reflected on my own experience as a black man in America and found solace in the adage: "That which does not kill me, makes me stronger." I continue to rise despite the obstacles of race, gender, and sexuality because they are the very sites of struggle from which I discover my strengths. My own personal struggle as an African-American man inspires and shapes "Gaze On Mandingo." The experience of engaging the questions that I pose here demonstrates one way that ethical experience can take the shape of an intellectual project. With each new discovery I make and with each question I encounter, I change my surroundings and my relationship to it. As I perform insurgent scholarship and as I accept the errors in judgment that reflect my naiveté, I am living. With each word that I write (and unwrite) I am consoled by the certainty that I can become. I am becoming!

---

10 In *Borderlands/La Frontera*, Gloria Anzaldúa defines La facultad as: "the capacity to see in surface phenomena the meaning of deeper realities, to see the deep structure below the surface. It is an instant 'sensing,' a quick perception arrived at without conscious reasoning . . . Those who do not feel psychologically safe or physically safe in the world are more apt to develop this sense. Those who are pounced on the most have it the strongest—the females, the homosexuals of all races, the darkskinned, the outcast, the persecuted, the marginalized, the foreign" (aunt lute books, San Francisco, 1987, page 38).

Breath 3

Queer Rhytes

Dear Book

Last night a man smiled at me. I liked him. Like I like my dad but am not supposed to. Like Sodom and Gom… well… that wicked city that is supposed to be an old time San Francisco: pink and evil. Men and women there are naked and they lust. Sounds exciting. I want to move there when I get big. Maybe there I will meet other blakkboys who had men smile at them and who liked it… the way the men pat their nappy heads. Maybe they went with the men like I did. The man who they trusted with me, who I trusted… I thought that he would love me. He was someone my daddy and momma knew. I have four other siblings, but he and his wife liked me the best. They said I smile nice. I try to frown when I smile so they both happen at the same time and my lips twist like I just bit a grapefruit.

We went to the house. The house smelled good. He and she had children of their own, but they were big. I wondered if he smiled at them like he did at me. Maybe I was special. I was scared to talk. I just tried not to smile. My dad said that sissies smile a lot and I don't want for him to know that I'm a sissy. Well… I play rough and have a hard punch, but daddy says that sissies like men. I like men. But I'm tough though. I like women too, but women don't hurt you so they can't love you as deep. They just love you and it's there. You just get used to it.

I keep seeing the Close-up commercial and I only see women and men, and they are always women and men of the same race kissing, and I asked my mom if love was the best thing to give, why Sodom was so bad? She said it was 'cause the Bible said so. Then I asked her what she thought. . . if she thought the same thing as the Bible thought. She said, "yes, I think what the Bible thinks." So I knew I couldn't tell her what the man who smiled at me did.

At first he was gentle. He had big hard-looking black hands but when he touched me, they felt smooth. I tingled. I knew that I was not supposed to like it, but I did. And he asked me to take off my clothes. I hate clothes. I took them off. His skin was brown just like me. I wanted to see his brown skin, but only big people can make little people take clothes off. He never took anything off. I wanted to see his brown skin. He was rubbing me on the head with his soft-hard hand. There was a glare in his eye and I knew he would protect me… like a father.

Then his other hand went down there… and back there… and he pushed his finger inside. It hurt, but I tried not to say anything. Big boys don't cry. Then the glare in his eyes changed. Then his hands didn't feel so soft anymore. He pushed deeper. I told him that it hurt. He told me to relax; said it shouldn't hurt. I had to remember what my dad said: Big boys don't cry. My dad is strong and black and meaner than them all. When I get bigger I will be tough like him. I will love a blakkboy and protect him. My dad was not there to protect me. Once in his sermon he said that faggots were an abomination. Then he told me once that I could talk to him about anything. Big people are stupid sometimes… and wrong a lot too.

I was crying that night, but only inside. I don't cry except for when I write in this book. I cried cause he pushed and then I started to feel like the inside of me was being cut up and it was hurting more when he pushed deeper. I cried out loud but without tears. Tears stopped coming after the first long minutes. Is this what love feels like? Maybe.

He turned me over and stuck my face in the pillow; but the rest of them in the house… they had to know. I could not breathe. All I could see was blackness. And I don't know if I was more scared of the blackness in the pillow or the man behind me with his weight on me. They had to know. No big person takes that long to tuck somebody else's blakkboy in. The black girl who was nice to me just before her daddy came in? She was smiling at me and we were singing: "Yes Jesus loves me… For the Bible tells me so." Then the man who smiled at me came in, her daddy. She stopped singing and her face changed. He told her to leave the room. She looked at me like she knew something I didn't. Maybe he loved her too?

My muffled screams were not loud enough. Sissies scream. Take it like a man. I don't talk about what happened except for in this here book. I don't want to go to hell for what we did. I wish love did not hurt.

I still wonder if there will ever be blakk men kissing each other in the Close-up commercials, except nice though. Not the way the man who smiled at me pushed his heavy lips on me. My dad said to stand up for what you believe, if you are a man. I believe that San Francisco is a nice place full of people who see Close-up commercials like I do. I don't believe that Jesus loves all the children of the world.

Does God's love hurt? Does he smile nice at his children… pat them on the head? Does he like the ones with funny looking smiles the best?

Goodnight, book. I have to go to bed. I will pray that I will forget the man and the night and what he did, so that I won't be afraid of blakk men when they smile nice at me. I want to be able to smile back—like I just bit a grapefruit; but with a tough grapefruit smile, not a sissy one.

unnatural acts

a damn trip
how some would rather see
his black fist
smashing teeth
gum-bleeding   and swollen
blakk skin
than witness
him caressing my hand
him lovingly stroking my face
'cause he felt like it
that moment
and could not wait
for the safety of closed quarters,
for our abysmal silence,
or for the blakk body-hiding night
to show love.

a damn trip
how some would prefer to see
cold   blakk   steel   barrel
pressed hard against G's temple
and a verbal exchange
that is
"I'll kill you, nigga!"
from one blakk man to another
whose response is
amplified heart beating
screaming for his life   in silence
and the tremble he hope not
set off
his grave.

some would prefer to see this
at cinemas or in hip hop video
than see dude's full brotha-like lips
pressed against
his lover's temple
soft and sweet-like
and hear the verbal exchange
"I love you, nigga!"
from one blakk man to another

whose response is
amplified heart beating
inside-screaming   'cause love is bliss
and him tremblin' 'cause
it's so brave to love
in this way
when blakk men are conditioned to
strike each other down
cut and bruise each other's
innocence
rather than protect it.

a damn trip. . . it is.
and I sometimes wonder
which acts some think
are most unnatural
blakk life ended
by the hands of another
blakk man
or life
cradled, kept, cherished
adored, made   safe.

About Radicalia Feminista
Phallacies and Queeries: A Phaggot's Contemplations

Radicalia Feminista proposes that men are themselves not liberated
and therefore cannot liberate women. I wholeheartedly agree. But I
sometimes wonder if we are even qualified to talk about men or wom-
en except to make reference to phony and dishonest categories that we
are made to believe are imperative and truthful. It is my belief that it
will not be men who liberate women nor women who will liberate
themselves, but a radically different species of ex-men and ex-women
who divest and agitate what "male" and "female" have come to signi-
fy. What I am interested in proposing is not some reunion of Yin and
Yang or the fusion of a male and female—happy mediums that are
grounded in refined lies. I'm not interested in rummaging through his-
tory to find some unsexed being who was free of a gender category.
Just how liberating can it be for us to all imagine ourselves as mothers
when mothering is so enmeshed in an opposition to fatherhood? Per-
haps we can all be sisters. For me, it is freer of significations than
mother. . . a designation that is all too contaminated for my bittersweet
tastes. Still, the sister becomes the wife and mother, so would we not
be burdened with freeing the sister that is still a she? Is this why the
some are eternally deconstructing his/story?

Radicalia Feminista doesn't seem to understand that there are those of
us who "pass," not necessarily for the other gender, but for the men
and women we are assumed to be. Will there be a struggle against
what we represent—men who refuse the illusions of manhood and
women who disidentify with femininity—when we cover a whole
range of gender appearances (some of which appear conventional)?
When amazons and the revolutionaries draw the swords to take off the
male heads, will I lose mine? Will they have non-deliberately executed
one of their warrior-allies? How can I protect myself if I am trapped in
this male body and my performance is not savvy enough to win favor
with the mothers; and when the fathers are the ones I have to defend
myself against? I'm concerned with finding ways to identify the men
(and women) who are allies but who will be mistaken for enemies.
Sometimes it gets confusing to try and figure out whether the warring
you do is killing off the enemies, the allies, or yourself.

Radicalia Feminista proposes that men learn total autonomy and that
we become "truly" rational beings. Indeed, male domination prefig-
ures a codependent relationship. Men dominate others when they
cannot control themselves. But what's up with this rite of passage

she requires of men like me—the burden of proving that I am not a tyrant like the others. I am presumed guilty until proven innocent. And the trial? Desert/shun? I already know those sands; tasted them when there was nothing else to eat. I recollect my thirst and hunger in equatorial temperatures as a personal testament of my survival. The desert's isolation can teach me autonomy and good sense no better than my own crowded ghetto streets.

I refuse to go into the desert to become a revolutionary unless I can bring the monsoon with me; unless my solitude can call forth kisses of ancestors who did not fit a gender, but who were made to fit one. There have to be rites of passage that don't require disconnection. I write and theorize in order to build a monument for the dead that re-casts them, not in the way some have come to know them—as men and women restricted to half-selves in order to secure the patriarchal order. I want to erect a monument for ancestors who wept and screamed (sometimes in secret and at other moments violently) be-cause of the burden between their legs and the tyranny that would define the rest of their lives because of it. It takes a brave soul to resist when resistance means death. That is why I forgive so many of the mothers and fathers before me—forgive them for their reluctant com-pliance to acting like a "real man" or "real woman." I thank those whose silent resistance eventually consumed them. I thank the witches and warlocks who screamed anyway and who were burned for it. I thank them for bequeathing just enough of the anti-sexed and vulnera-ble spirit in them to me so that I would be more aware and better able to forge resistance.

Some of the feminists have written men wrong. Rather, what they write about men seems so non-representative of me. I have never ac-cepted manhood; and most of my life have represented, only in form, that gender that is both defined by my biological constitution and a socially prescribed performance. Masculinity. Masks. I mastered them well enough to be marked as male. I am a double-crosser. Have al-ways disturbed masculinity. I am a faggot/traitor to the male sex because I do not long to possess a woman. Many black women say that I am a waste and not a real man because I do not accept my right-ful position as head of the black family. I refuse to donate sperm to replenish the earth with male (or female) revolutionaries who beat their wives. I want to raise anti-boys and anti-girls.

I held on for dear life to that vulnerability little boys are comfortable with until they are told that the feeling is reserved only for women and to maintain order. I am told that this emotionally exposed position is women's handicap. I infer that women's vulnerability is why men have believed that they are naturally qualified to rule over women. I do not welcome that lie, nor do I want any part in the self-deception. I refuse to associate with men who exploit women in order to make the lies seem worth it.

Freud was such a punk. They idolize his prescriptions. Dora should have owned a gun.

Men cloak the lack with violence. Each time he strikes her body or spirit he is further removed from that frightened boy within himself who fears that his weakness will be uncovered. He reiterates the violence enough to himself and to women so that they too will come to believe that the lack has been erased—that his vulnerability has been undone. The tyrant is nothing more than a punk who compulsively bluffs. Feminist Patricia Robinson was right. The tyrant must convince his subjects that he is a god, not vulnerable. But there is a problem. Each strike, rather than erasing the vulnerability, comes to signify it all the more. So some try to reduce the effects or intensity of the blow with kinder and more gentle acts of violence that do not scar the body. Economic and social scars sometimes cut as deep but we can ignore the wounds for they can be construed as having origins which have nothing to do with sexist violence: capitalism or women's oblivion to the small strides given to them. I liked that about Feminist Firestone. She calls Marx out on his blatant oversight. Stabilize the classes and there will still be a need for battered women's shelters.

Vulnerability for some boys is such a terrifying bottomless pit that they strike relentlessly at everything, believing that even death and war and the battle scars are better than living with the "lack" that is open, fluid, innocent, peaceful...is genesis. That which some have come to regard as woman (the feminine), does not struggle against this "lack" to save her life. This is not the "feminine" script that men wrote for women to make them forget the vulnerability underneath their performances of mother, wife, daughter, whore. Some women have come to understand that they are being programmed to forget and hate the "lack" and are warring to get it back. This is a different kind of violence than the one men (and women frightened into docility) reiterate; for it is violence for and not against what is essential and true. Humans are essentially vulnerable; a lack and possibility that is never filled.

Then there are boys who are the anti-men men. Not those who do parodies on the feminine but who fix it all the more in doing so: the cross dressers who desire to be "real women." There are men who do a parody on manhood, and who appear to be men. Exemplary mimicry. But is it mimicry if it is mistaken for something real? I presume that our satirical mastery of manhood is precisely why many of us have escaped being put to death. We terrify other boys because we infiltrate and mock masculinity. We are butch dykes with biological penises that we do not exalt. We refuse the primacy and supremacy given to the phallus but will use it to "screw" the man. Acting manly and having a cock makes it harder for the patriarchs to identify the traitor-men and so we sometimes bark and pout and be afraid right alongside them just enough not to forget that they are wimps. We don't pity them. They have always had the option of being a different kind of man, but like the benefits that come with patriarchy. They are my enemies even when they are the lovers of my sisters or brothers.

My pops might have become a male traitor. But he was weak and frail and afraid to bash his pops in the head for fear that he would get the beating reserved for his moms. He was weaker than the mother who beat him and locked him in closets without food. But he escaped and was taught the brutality that is the only option for broken ghettoboys. Hardness was and is still a pervasive untruth. It is spoken and spoken and spoken again in technosynthetic winds so much that many of us boychildren no longer recognize its bitter sting in the throat or the way it makes our eyes tear. We are desensitized; crying without tears and believing that we cry for no reason.

Uncle Sam say: "Punk." "Sissy." "Faggot." Pops wiped his tears away with knife blades and gun barrels. They did not absorb his pain. The tears just rolled off in Vietnam and on the Southside of Chicago. He forgot his tenderness and became his father. And my father? Cycle. I someday want to hear his story of fear and self-loathing. I have tried to love him even when he has been abusive. Sometimes I am not sure how to love him when he is courageous enough to try and love me. I long to be a father– differently and similarly– recognizing the sweetness that came out of bitterness. It is all that I have.

Some of my allies are queer boys who are aware of the pitiful state of men—who know that women have been exploited because men are weaker beings and are not brave enough to live with weakness. Often women learn to cultivate this tenderness . . . except for the girls who scream because they should not be punished for being essentially human, essentially vulnerable. These are women who, like Audre Lorde, tell the truth about themselves even when death tries to steal them away. They are prophets.

Most girls grow tired of fighting the order of things, as prescribed by capitalist, patriarchal society. Women too wear masks. My grandma, the Cherokee Indian, she did; and was still driven mad. They say lots of Indian women are mad. As if there are not reasons why this might be the case.

I have learned that it is sometimes easier to wear masks and perform the designated roles; much harder to perform your way out of the script by inventing something new and not yet experienced. I have re-iterated maleness just enough to get by. At times, I have felt trapped and have tried to find others like myself. Not those boys who, seeing the evil done to women after the lady doth too aggressively protest, decide to become more sensitive patriarchs. I have wanted to meet the boys who never "bought" the lie in the first place: that there was so much to gain from covering that lack which is vulnerability with our fists and howls and guns and bombs.

I cannot understand Radicalia Feminista and her voice. It screams an appropriated-half/woman-man-trapped in defensive but anxious Western philosophy. Philosophy will have no part with what she is attempting to do, and so the words backfire and come out contorted. I have two philosophy degrees but refuse to write like that anymore. I don't believe that she really sounds like that. She makes no sense when she talks about sexual intercourse and even less sense when she talks about lesbians. Lesbianism can be incredibly political and subversive. Not the kind of lesbianism that Feminist Lila Karp talks about—the category created by Freud and his boys for their sexual kicks. Like the heterosexed female homosexuality where women strike each other and one is the breadwinner.

I experienced being a lesbian once. My girlfriend wouldn't let me use my penis and it fucked with my head. I became more fully human and experienced a more fully eroticized body as a result. Marcuse and Deleuze said that this could happen. My girlfriend and I explored polymorphous perversities and I was fine with being completely vulnerable with her. She even entered me once and I wasn't afraid. But her girlfriends suspected that I was a fag-patriarch trying to convert an amazon . . . and eventually it got to her . . . and she left. But my being with her in that way was political . . . and not: it was because we violated the sodomy laws and not because her making love to me just was . . . nothing complicated. Not the result of feuding parents or teen rebellion, but an openness that is there in everyone but which I did not deny. Is that what lesbianism is? An openness and not a concealment? Many feminists don't understand. They have read too much Freud. They call him out for the lies he told, but he appears in their writing and analysis, laughing at his success. Feminist Lila Karp should have been more careful when she entertained his Three Essays on the Theory of Sexuality. It is fiction.

The ironic thing about reiterating the gendered performance is that one can begin to believe that the performance is real. Ironically, he or she must keep performing it so that the lie will not be exposed. Unfortunately, there are women and men who continue to do violence to the truth of the body each time they deny its vulnerability. But there is an agitated army of radical cloaking traitors just waiting to "come out"— a tribe of Judases who never bought that Jesus was king of kings. . . Just a genderless spirit: vulnerable and wanting.

Java Script
(or why I no longer "SLAM")

I cannot breathe inside of this blackness
the thick of java scripts is madd dense.
revolutionary lips spit dream themes nostalgic.
memory lapse supplanted by hand claps.
body postures dramatize
'cause words don't move
don't create mood
don't challenge
just corroborate the same ole same bullshit
'bout a revolution you look for
in some Afrocentrist's history book,
re-rehearsed till it cooks your cerebrum.
humdrum lyric bout "*black* when we were kings"
and now we just bling bling!!!
nigga please?!

no longer pushed or moved or panthered
by melanin theories or the original sin stories 'bout devils
or how some white patriarch
made me a black phaggot
I look to my reflection at mirrors for my third eye
looking back blacker than your black.
I fell in love with myself like Narcissus
java scripts defied, defiled
for the very blakk truth of my affections
predilections: self inscription
on country tree bark torn apart
by mills.
pines converted to paper
still afford my rhytes to nature.

i gots a body rock warmed by "Lovers Rock"
and know postmodern panthers in high heels
blitzin' bashers on 14th and Broadway.

cuz soon after I was born
my enemy appeared right before me
the moment he said I had to be
just like him
blakk like that . . . I found that wack.

no longer seduced by macho rhytes of passage
got flack . . . so that's that.
suffocated and frustrated by 2x4's
and nailed to an assimilationist's crucifix
I freed myself the night I tasted
my first tongue kiss
dreadlocks deadlocked in cowry clips
I chopped
breath shortened by head locks.

no longer allowing blackness to remain
an inferno
obscuring my halo
suppressing the G.O.D. in me
L.O.V.E. said to me
to stop readin' poems pretendin'
with false pronouns
gesturing normality.

I be a queer abstract black cat
galactically placed at margins
to keep the center together.
black aristocrats can't never define my black . . .
it's mine.
done worn it for 28 years on this black back
and via ancestral revolutions:
black generations under attack

my revolution starts here.
don't need no damn kufi to speak for me.
conjugated my own Ebonics,
critically absorb rebel words for just wars.
I come for humdrum black trapped in incense sticks,
smothering under headwraps, oils frankincense,
loud lips spitting rebel rifts,
just to vent cause java scripts
got me incensed.

no longer hiding behind metaphysics
and discursive terse verses
self reveals self: vulnerable but headstrong
reflection eternal.
self-inspection always and forever fertile.

Jupiter

s/he be southren crunk with juju beads
and layered accessories
furs, African headwraps worn as skirts
a jigsaw collage
personified as poetry
boundless energy that stall eyeballs
but s/he don't care that you watchin'
don't have time to notice
s/he knows you look
predicted it in his/her crystal disco ball
after first conferin' with Ms. Cleo,
Badu and amber incense sticks.

his/her apple tree grow persimmons and peaches
and s/he don't mind
pluck'em all the same
like Pat Metheny refrains
like Coltrane horny for abstraction
s/he is a neither/nor either/or
which you shouldn't mind, because s/he don't
stop to sweat crooked stairs.
s/he be that deep amorphous hurricane
screaming at asteroids
to "back the fuck up!"
with a Gloria Gaynor remix
as his/her backgroove
s/he grooves black, shuffles
and them eyes glimmer fab.

his/her tongue is androgynous
choosing not to choose English over Ebonics
but marrying them where the tongue
meets the gum.
cataclysmic galactic angel
s/he be
the intensity of a nebula . . . glowing
falling until one catches what remains
a thousand years later
in the sting of a winter wind
or a summer heat monkey wave.

s/he is brave to be, to live
courageous-like
so punks try to punk him/her
just to find their manhood
disrupted and shivering;
their reflections cast
in a shiny hammer head.

A Letter to Hélène Cixous

My comrade Cixous,

eye address you as such because I deplore your other name—the one
that looks like Helen. It is fixed and reminds me of other things:

> mothers who were mothered to be mothers
> and nothing else
> daughters who did not resist
> blind, sympathetic female characters
> naive television girlchildren
> who happily went about picking lilies and berries in the fields
> and who did not suspect the conquering of dark peoples
> by their fathers
> or the passivity of their mothers.

This name 'Cixous' is both "new" and "nothing" to me. I find solace
and freedom in that . . . a name which does not remind—which alludes
to that space my tongue prevents me from knowing: the space I can
attach no meaning to. 'Cixous' sustains the symbolism only my pre-
linguistic self understands. I died when eye spoke and so I seek re-
birth. My own words turned against me the very moment I uttered
them.

> 'Cixous': such a cool name. Suoxic would be just as cool!

Who is this eye that I speak of—who inspects you so closely— who
addresses you with such emancipated opinion? eye hesitate to name
myself, as you might find my name deplorable too, Cixous. Would it
remind? And what might you associate it with (in any of your
tongues)?

> man? woman? activity? passivity?
> darkness? light? culture? nature?

None of the above? Would you entertain the possibility of me being
one of your warrior-friend he-she allies? Will you allow me participa-
tion in your army?

I write you because it's much easier than reading you. I envy your en-
durance. The bizarre fluidity of your words confuse me. You do not
struggle against the I. You insert it as your own, and thus, your crafty

manipulation of words protects against the enemies. I write you as a way of engaging your method, honing my own rebel strategy. I want for my words to make love to me in the way yours do for you. I wish to insert an 'other' you do not fear, will not war against. Will replacing a phallocentric, suspect, dialectical model with one that explores the possibility of trust disarm the unavoidable war between you and eye? Pardon the questions. eye've heard all my life that I have a tendency to ask too many questions, Cixous. I feel you will not require an apology for probing questions. This I trust you will feel. Will you allow me this anti-agonistic space? Will you defer suspecting me for the moment?

My knowledge of you seems to rest on the assumption that you already identify with the mad expression of my muthatongue. But for me to assume such an identification with you, to claim any such knowledge of you, is to confine you, un-Cixous you, play scramble with your name, so that you fit somewhere in the very binary I claim to resist. But your resistance amazes me, Cixous! For neither ixousc, xousci, ouscix, or uscixo make sense to me. How liberating it must be to have such a name!

eye permanently defer any speculation that my comrade, you are not. For you, eye destruct the urge to continue confusing the I. Eye will tell you who I am because U have told me who you are. You are: the warrior whose language marks her country, whose first resistance is post-colonial, whose very identity opposes any stabilization of identity or language—and so much more. Can this mutual recognition of the other-powers we distrust and other-vulnerabilities we recognize be a method that assists in deconstructing the binary oppositions we fight? Do I repeat the same questions? Help me understand! If I resist the phallocentric urge to view you as an othering 'other' might you also see me differently, non-agonistically? And yet, it seems that if I do not resist you, make war against the power you can use to 'other' me, then I might allow myself to be obliterated. Is this why you "have always wanted war"? I war because I fear! Fear seems to perpetuate and sustain the binary. But is it reasonable, possible, to live without fear? How do you war without killing off allies? This frustrates me!

You say:

> I come biographically, from a rebellion, from a violent and
> anguished direct refusal to accept what is happening on the

stage on whose edge I find I am placed, as a result of the combined accidents of History. ("Sorties, "[11] 70)

"A result of combined accidents of HIStory" I feel I am too. Tim'm. Violent. Accident. The unveiling of that name was inevitable, Cixous. I cannot employ such strategized silence-speak much longer if I sincerely want to help you fight the war. Tim'm. What does it mean for you? Does it upset? Does it remind you of biblical apostles you conveniently omitted when you "took short cuts" through your skimming of the Bible?

> White male prophet
> whose words signify things
> like death and suffering
> for folk like me.
> Book of life?!
> Rather it is white man
> whose words are taken to mean
> what those who conquer assert.

(I cannot use these words, Cixous. They are too corrupted!)

> I don't feel no connection to that Timothy character!
> He's too knowable.
> They trapped him in a book
> and he can be nothing beyond their translation of him.

Please forgive my occasional renouncing of proper speech. When impassioned my natura-tongue tends to reveal other linguistic sensibilities and wits. This accidental tongue is sassy and come from thick, full lips, and mos' time don't make no sense to folk who try too hard to translate.

You "learned to read, to write, to scream, and to vomit in Algeria" (Sorties, 70). That you recall so much of this place, this Algeria, elicits envy in me! You seem to have an access to the origin of your resistance unavailable to me. Cincinnati ain't nothin' but a word on my birth certificate. But I've heard stories from mutha 'bout what I was like then:

> mutha-strength provided an 'easy' birth.

---

[11]
Sorties is among the essays in the critically acclaimed "The Newly Born Woman. Hélène Cixous and Catherine Clément. Translation by Betsy Wing. Theory and History of Literature, Volume 24. University of Minnesota Press. 1986

They all noticed a horrifying reluctance on my part
to scream like most babies—
until doctor tried to cut off my clit.
It was then that I put up fit!

I still maintain the foreskin which dulled the blade
and skin of femininity maintain.
(I still resist, Cixous!)
In Cincinnati, she wanted to name me Toya.
I came out a boy,
but mutha say Timothy was as good as a boyish boy
as any woman wanting a girl could want.

quiet
she say I seldom cried out or screamed or vomited,
(like you did, Cixous.)
I banged on the high-chair when hungry
and applesauce quieted me
the forbidden fruit still tantalizes, satisfies,
massages my tongue,
prepares it for rebellious speech.

My first word was "dagum" and mutha say I was trying to signify a
father . . . who was seldom around. Rather problematic, don't you
think, Cixous? Dagum ----->Dad? Oh, but an innate, intrinsic longing
(say Freud), to identify with father-power/phallic destiny, forced such
words right?

Mistranslation

I don't know nothing else of Cincinnati 'cept my inability to spell it
right (unless, by chance I stop resisting long enough to conform to cor-
rect spellings, good vernacular, proper speech). I learned to bang on
high-chairs and be misunderstood in Cincinnati. I think that I learned
how to read, write, scream, and vomit elsewhere. I did learn!

You say:

So I am three or four years old and the first thing
I see in the street is that the world is divided in half,
organized hierarchically, and that it maintains this
distribution through violence. ("Sorties, " 70)

eye saw this too! Dagum, whose participation in 'family' was sporadic, dominated. He was a preacher who talked a lot and seldom meant anything he said. He was crafty with words, and this I admired . . . even though the words sometimes wounded. But it was his ruling by the fist that I feared most. It silenced mutha and yet beat her for not speaking. Hands choked her so that she had no breath to speak. It struck the blow to mutha—which ignited baby screams—and shook babies in mid air for being noisy. Dicktator!

He was powerful, domineering, tyrannical, ugly: MAN.

He was me ten times bigger, Cixous. I hated this! Male destiny being played to me before innocent "I's." A boychild as young as I could not turn off the recording—would never be able to disable the brain's tendency to recall. I hated the nightmares in the middle of the day! Cixous, I wanted desperately to resist this destiny. I wanted to understand where the aspiration to resist originated, so that I could take my mind back there and get more resistance-substance.

Most boys knew it made little sense to resist such destinies (privileges) and did not hesitate to strike the little girls (and boys) who were too afraid to strike back. Boys were mean! I resisted boydom. I resist feeling dis tiny. How do rebel boychildren survive, Cixous? Will I have to find my own way? I recall these words of yours:

> There has to be some "other" —no master without a slave, no economico-political power without exploitation, no dominant class without cattle under the yoke, no Frenchmen without wogs, no Nazis without Jews, no property without exclusion—an exclusion that has its limits and is part of the dialectic. ("Sorties, " 71)

Is 'othering' really inevitable and unavoidable, Cixous? I had hoped that there was another way, but it seems like there will always be 'othering.' Our struggle is an ardent search for that unexploitative, antiexclusionary, non-dialectical space where my 'othering' you is non-antagonistic.

My mutha gave birth to Toya, my lil sista. I sometimes wonder if I was supposed to be her and she me, or the both of us indistinguishable—both with affinities for whatever color boyblue and girlpink make when they consolidate. What color would that be?

In the dark or in closets or in the ghetto alley, Toya and I exchanged blues for pinks and white Barbies for green army trucks. These were secret spaces where resisting, where the nurturing of rebel consciousness, was encouraged. But then we got caught by Dagam.

"There will be no faggots or bulldaggers in the house of a man of God!"

So sista and I stopped resisting for fear of fist-powers. And when I named myself I stuttered, out of fear: "Tim m mm m mm m". Where did I learn such fear? How did I grow to fear resistance? And the children joked: "Tim and m and mm and m."

Cixous,

If only I had words to express my hatred for their trivialization of my impediment. But mutha taught me somethin' bout not letting words hurt me: "sticks and stones may break my bones but w w w words will n n nnever hurt me." And they did! Mutha was wrong. Lil' Timothy wanted to die—die too weak to rebel, too scared to speak, but at least having learned to strike at those who angered him. Die a boy. This broad-shouldered stocky lil' boychild found it terribly difficult to resist any longer. And sista Toya and I stopped playing together. Violent inaction.

And so I lived a boy! Turned over desks in furious rages when "punks" looked at me the wrong way. Destiny. Talked loud like Dagam and intimidated others by biting and scratching and hitting those who challenged my mask-you-linity. I masked. Is this how Dagam got the way he is? Did he lack the strength to resist?

Cixous,

Where did you acquire your strength? Your girlchild seems so much stronger than my boychild. No less conscious of how violence attacks, however. Where did you get your armor?

> You say:
>
> I asked everywhere: where does your strength come from? What have you done with your power? What cause have you served? ("Sorties, " 73)

Did anyone answer you, Cixous? How did you connect with "the persons endowed with an individual strength but without authority"? (Sorties, 73)

The play and exchange between you and me must be one strategy we can employ in order to connect—connect with anti-agonistic warrior-speaks, like self. I responded with a Dagam-like black churchy Amen when you said:

> Everyone knows that a place exists which is not economically or politically indebted to all the vileness and compromise. That is not obliged to reproduce the system. That is writing! If there is somewhere else that can escape the infernal repetition, it lies in that direction, where it writes itself, where it dreams, where it invents new worlds. ("Sorties, " 72)

My knee-jerk skepticism of the agency writing-armor "guarantees" temporarily subsided the day I affirmed "Tim'm." Speech therapy would not cause me to forget or deny the name that signifies both of my death and re-birth. Rebirth! Tim'm! I speak "properly" now, except for the sounding of my name.

My strength was revitalized by a growing awareness of muthabuse. How many of my siblings were born out of (consensual) lovemaking by my parents? Was I (rapechild)? Does it matter, Cixous? How many whitefolk at grocery stores will sneer at my mutha's use of foodstamps to feed her seven children? I wanted to kill them for their hatred! This is when I first understood the binary, Cixous.

        cash/foodstamps
        white/black
        rich/poor
        power/impotence

These binaries are not so subtle. And there are others. Violence!

"Why did your mother have so many children?" the sem-pathetic white lady asked

Violence. If I knew words better then, I woulda said: "Maybe it wadn't her choice." Fighting Back. Talking Back. Tim'm! Names aren't supposed to have apostrophes!

Cixous,

I don't like war! I wanted to believe that change would arrive by having "peace talks"—the kind white men who run the world create for each other because peaceful talk is not a given. Violence. Upon reading of your obsession with this battle I wanted to scream: "You are wrong! You cannot fight violence with violence." But I realized early that there is a difference between the type of violence which aims to kill those with less power and the violence one assumes to save her life. I learned to read and rhyte to save my life!

> if I myself shout in disgust, if I can't be alive without being angry, there must be others like me. I don't know who, but when I'm big, I'll find them and I'll join them. ("Sorties, " 72)

That I have too mouthed those very words must represent something. Coalition? Ally? Friend?

I had lots of friends as a child: Dr. Seuss, Webster (and his dick-son, airy), Sesame Street. I manipulated and re-invented their intent in order to arm myself. I admired genderless puppets and cartoons and solicited their help against nightmares. We successfully joined forces and battled nightmares in the way I wish to conspire against the enemy with you, Cixous.

I asked my fear of other to go somewhere and hide, so that I could write you. Every reading of your words invents a new text for me. Differently revolutionary. You inspire strategies for boychildren like myself who resist—bisexual, enigmatic, spiritually hermaphroditic souls who learn to war in order to end war. The newly born woman you represent encourages me to find a space where new men can be born.

We will subvert and substitute old binaries for new ones, I submit an example of this new binary, this new 'othering.' Strong rebellious names grounded in painful but resilient personal-narratives. An unassuming sharing 'tween U and eye secures the new model: What might resemble?

Cixous/Tim'm?

Breath 4

Dis/Ease

Suicide Journal

It was never meant for me to be born here. I was supposed to remain an angel—sliding around Saturn's rings, skinny-dipping in Jupiter's hurricane, making sandcastles on the moon. Instead, somebody's selfish prick forced itself into a fertile womb world . . . and again, and again . . . and eventually, I arrived. There are others who came like this. We are unlike others here, without predilection for sensibility, without eyes that intuit, without lips that spit the unspeakable. Sometimes recognized early as bright or special or a little queer, we were meant to wander the earth scribbling graffiti on the beds of rivers or on redwood bark.

I have almost drowned. I have almost been run over on an Arkansas dirt road by rebel-flag rednecks. I have been raped till I bled. I have been spiritually tormented trying to fit into places where I was never welcome. There are others: Hansberry, Baldwin, Basquiat, Newton, Riggs, Joan of Arc, Deleuze, Foucault, some unnamed, bad-mouthed Creole, country girl in Appalachia or the Black Belt. Twenty-seven years after my father and some doc interpellated me as a boy (which I don't believe I am . . . not a girl either . . . why do our genitals dick/tate?) I am beginning to notice my period: gonorrhea blood-drip on the undees. I am feeling queasy and pregnant with babies named Crixivan, Zerit, and Viramune. I want to abort them! They are not natural and leave me feeling synthetic.

Is there a place outside of this psycho ward that is safe for us? I have found a few: a dance floor cracking heartbeat house music, a glance across the room at some chocolate boy who wonders what is so striking about the brown-Indian with deep-cut eyes besides his look back. This hospital room is a safe sanctuary. There is no dis/ease here. No black family member disgusted with your perversity, no selfish administrator or bureaucrat with a dead/line disguised under a compliment like: "you are so talented!"

I want to collect some of the shit I've written; compile the journal I could never fully commit to but that is patiently strung together by my tears. I cannot cry anymore. I can only find solace in my madness, my eccentricity, my dis/ease and a hope that there is some basis for connection with others. I want to commingle the mad scribblings with the conventional ones; dis-identification will be the subtext. I am always necessarily becoming something I am not yet aware of. My tribe? We embody transition. Stagnation and traditions make us vomit. We don't mind admitting our fuck-ups or disclosing our traumas. Disclosure of this sort is our expression of freedom and one of the ways we connect with our own. My tribe? If you gotta ask, then nigga, you don't know. And all in my tribe is my niggas: females, shemales, girlymen, boy-boys, Chinese, Caribbean, and Polish alike.

I once thought that I would find salvation in Africa-motherland dirt. I would drink it and would be spared a genealogical memory I do not wish to own: lynchings, what it feels like to be gunned down by cops or my own peeps wearing a different color head rag, or my head pushed down in some pillow while somebody spills they seed in my hole. My tribe? We lure Holocausts and Middle Passages and executions and lynchings and rapes because we threaten those who want to promote the idea that heaven is after and not now, up there and not here. We want to make it happen here. There is nowhere else for us. We have already been angels! Capitalism and starvation and dis/ease and war and hate are acceptable as long as there is an afterlife. I want to kiss a Korean baby on her forehead and call her my lil' ghetto-daughter, teach a bagpipe player how to accompany a DJ scratch. Teach "straights" and "gays" that there are no such things. Fictions on which traditions are based prevent our inalienable freedom. I have never believed that it was meant for me to be here for very long. I have been bleeding on the insides for years and have concealed or ignored the discomfort of internal ruptures.

I am in a psych unit, twenty-seven years (and then some) after I pushed myself out, screaming. Sometimes I still raise hell. Back in the day, mama said I banged on high chairs and contemplated cartoons. Now I beat djembes and theorize this theater that is life. I still believe this here earth could be heaven. Complacent, humans give up on this too easily. Make excuses for things gone wrong: hate, injustice, suffering, hunger. If only others like me weren't snuffed out so early. We must really be dangerous to the order of things. Sometimes this ultimate belief in our personal freedom has meant condomless fucking, a poem for every day of the week, coping with our own dynamic alterity, or helping others be patient enough to love our differences and recognize their own insanities.

I want to string together a web of notes where teardrops meet the page and form alphabets. I want for these soul droppings to be brave enough to assemble words I dare say or write. I want to be courageous enough to accept that I am not "just like everyone else" nor do I ever want to be. I want to create a suicide journal, before the event, that I can read and be afraid of the consequences . . . and not follow through. I want suicide notes that sing soprano and baritone at once—meshing into the praisesong my belly wails when it rumbles. There in the gut, where I beg for more strength to put up with what lies outside of this hospital window, I want to solicit an army of writing rebels . . . whose optimism and hope for heaven on earth is as sensible as a suicide journal: volatile, full of passion, wishing to be found before the exit, a daily manifesto for salvation.

Letter to Mom

Mom and the fam,

It's seldom that I write you a letter. I usually reserve letters for words my lips fail to pronounce, unspeakable things . . . or at least things that are difficult to talk about. I want to thank and acknowledge you for your understanding around my HIV/AIDS status. I should remind you that I'm fast-improving. My number of T-cells (fighter cells) are increasing, the amount of virus is decreasing. There is not yet a cure. No matter how low the amount of virus in my body gets, even if it is undetectable by certain methods, I am not cured. But with medication and good physical and psychological health, I can maintain a full and healthy life. With new and better medications each day, I'm hoping to be around for a lot longer. But this is the easy stuff to talk about. I have enclosed a brochure that you might find informative.

Now . . . the hard stuff to talk about.

I am gay—a fact that I shared with you almost ten years ago, but one which you still may have not accepted or come to terms with. It hasn't been a phase . . . I was gay long before I ever said a word about it to you. I was gay when I acted out in strangely silent and depressed ways that only the creator had answers for. I was gay when I threw myself so deeply into my studies because I realized that life in Taylor, Arkansas, was killing my spirit. Grandma said to always tell the truth. I wished that she would have warned that people wouldn't always reward you for the truth. Sometimes people deny the truth, hide from it, make believe it is something other than what it is. I needed to be free to love. As a more volatile young adult, I had been tricked to think I could change my homosexual feelings. Indeed, I could pretend the life of a heterosexual . . . this could only be a performance that would deny me of my truest feelings. As a teen, I could never feel the passion for women that I did for men. I can't explain it. I don't even try anymore. That said, I can be understanding of—but cannot feel what it is like—to be sexually drawn or attracted to a woman or a heterosexual marriage. This tirade seems so elementary and I should stop, as I've probably said this before or you are already aware of my position on this issue.

But the context of these ramblings has changed. True, I contracted HIV/AIDS from a homosexual partner. I'm not entirely sure whom. I have an idea, but every time I try to pin it down I realize that I putting energy into a task that won't change my status or make me feel any better about things. AIDS exists. It's an unfortunate fact for us all: black, white, gay, straight, or anything in-between. I believe, as you do, that the Bible is against homosexuality. But unlike you, I don't believe everything in the Bible, nor do I claim to be Christian (though I acknowledge my roots in the Christian church and its role in grounding me spiritually). When I decided to affirm my sexual orientation as a gay, I reasoned that I couldn't claim both Christianity and homosexuality. I chose the identity I was born with rather than the identity I was indoctrinated into. As I see it, I was born black, a male, and gay . . . none of these I could change (well . . . that's not entirely true in this surgery-obsessed/change-what-you-don't-like world we live in . . . but I don't believe in changing things given to me by the creator). I am a man who is proud of and non-apologetic about this decision, despite some of its consequences—the worst of which might have been a lonely and confused past filled with not so good judgments about relationships. The best of which is to follow:

I am HIV positive, I'm twenty seven, and I'm in love. August Byron Oakman, my partner and friend, is among the best things I've been blessed with. He is sensitive, warm, understanding, patient. He takes good care of your son, Irma. We have a relationship that is not obsessed with sexual attraction (as the Christian Right might think), in part because we are currently separated by the state of Oregon (he lives near Seattle, WA), but primarily because, more than anything, I value his friendship and his willingness to work, each day, to be a better partner. Our relationship has developed fast—so much that we were initially overwhelmed by it all. Now we just accept it as what it is: unexplainably beautiful. We take things day by day . . . enjoying the moments we have with each other and working towards a future together. Don't get me wrong, August is more than a special or close friend. We are intimate with each other . . . it's the natural expression of romantic love between people who care, as we do, about each other. I know that I want to spend as long as I have on this earth reciprocating all that he gives to me that is beautiful: the unconditional love, the hope for a happy home and family, a true system of support (maybe even some grandkids for you . . . right now there is at least Silky, the beautiful pooch in the picture I have sent). (smile) It's interesting to me that lots of heterosexual relationships often don't have these supportive qualities and yet by virtue of their resemblance to Adam and

Eve, all is OK . . . even if it is an abusive or terribly dysfunctional relationship. So much of why I'm happy, optimistic, and motivated has to do with the security and faith I have in my relationship with August. Indeed more important is my faith in a creator who blesses this relationship and who would give me strength if I didn't have the support of a partner. But right now I have some help with getting through this muddle that is life . . . and that's nice.

I wanted to share this because I know that it's easier to deal with Timothy Terrell when he's single (and perhaps even lonely)—that then there is at least the hope that he might change or convert to the righteous way of wife and kids—while the pronouncement or declaration of my love for a same-sex partner is a lot harder to manage. My relationship somehow makes the homosexuality more permanent, a lot more difficult to ignore. My partner and I make plans together, we are patiently building a life together in faith. This is something that I've never had. I've wanted it. I've convinced myself at times that I had it. But nothing like this. I am as sure of my love for August (and his for me) as I am of my strange childhood liking for "ketchup on my cornbread." I don't ask that you like my homosexuality or my partner's. I no longer expect that. What I do ask is that you respect my decision as an adult to build the best and happiest life for myself. My cousin Cynthia once declared that she would appreciate it if I would fulfill her dream of me building a heterosexual family. The angry part of me wanted to ask that she fulfill a few of my dreams for her, starting with . . . But I love and respect the decisions she's made for herself and her family, even as I may disagree with some of them. I wonder if she realized how ridiculous her request sounded. She might as well have said: "I don't care about your own happiness; you have a duty to live in a manner that I will be happy with." Our families will always want certain things for us in life, but they also have to come to terms with the decisions we make as adults. I don't live my life to make the Stinsons happy, though I certainly hope that I make them happy and proud.

As an alternative I suppose that I could revert to that closet behavior and be right back in that suicidal and depressed state that almost cost my life as a teen. The ability to love freely is a God given right. We want for those who are closest to us to share our joy of love. I hope to be "married" someday too. I won't expect the support that Cynthia received when she married. That's the reality that I live with and terms which I accept. But you have to understand that if August continues to be the jewel in my life that he is to me today, it's kind of a package deal; a Tim'm West-Oakman kind of thing.

August and I are not yet "married," and you don't have to worry about us upsetting Christmas dinner, but there will be times in the future that I will come home and he will be with me, as anyone's primary support system is expected to do. I am thankful that his family appears to be receptive to the idea of someone in his life who supports and cares about him; who continues to bring him happiness.

We share with those we love most the best things we find. When I was a kindergarten student, I returned home with a huge bag of potato chips from Nelson potato chip factory. It was then that I realized that my intelligence could help put food on a family's table. I zipped home with my Batman (or was it Spiderman?) raincoat and our little hungry, poverty-stricken family got full on flat-fried starch that night. (smile). I remember that dilapidated house on the hill. I remember eating peanuts for a couple of days because dad wasn't providing and you were too proud to ask for help. We made it work anyway. We shared and sacrificed and made things stretch.

I am sharing with you now, years later, something I have found that fills my spirit with happiness, in these difficult times. Nothing is certain between August and me, but I have faith in us. I also have faith that my family will find the wherewithal to dig deep for a little respect and strength to get beyond what others might think, what they will say, how this might reflect on your rearing (which I must say, given my many perfectly heterosexual siblings, it hasn't). (smile)

Mother, you are amongst the most important people in my life. I don't know how much time these meds will buy me . . . hopefully a lifetime . . . but nothing is certain. I wake to thank God for each day and each opportunity I get to share a piece of myself with you. I want for you to be proud of me, not selectively: applauding the degrees and accomplishments but embarrassed and ashamed about that which brings me so much joy and support. I don't know that I've ever been this frank with you. It's always been difficult; and my hesitation might well be me projecting insecurities onto you. If my own fear has prevented you from getting to know your son better, I am sorry. There are times when you will defer the truth to keep things together, so to speak. And there comes a time when the truth has to prevail; whether we like the truth or not.

I love you. That's the truth. I want for our family to become as close as we were crowded at 1320 Monroe or at 1220 Columbia 18. That's the truth. I'm coming home for Christmas and am happy about it (details to follow). That's the truth. Unfortunately, I'm making the trip without August . . . but there's always the next time. Will the family respect me enough to not expect me to keep silent about my life while others comfortably boast their husbands, wives, boyfriends, girlfriends, children? I'm not sure. But this is something that we will have to confront together as a family if I am to feel comfortable making return visits. All the shame and silence, on top of the financial stresses, make it easier to just stay away longer. The man I have become does more with his life than teach, perform, and write. I fall out of and in love, I get sad and lonely, I worry about my sibs, I miss my mommy and aunts and uncle and cousins. This is the all of me I hope you will patiently grow to accept. Time will tell. Love is patient.

Love your big baby boy,

Tim'm Terrell West

Ceremonies
(for Essex)

on the other side of what I don't know
is what I know.
my bedroom, a shrine
and the feelings poured into it:
evaporated tear-droplets
a smile trapped still in some photo,
love potions, sea shells, a fortune cookie script,
and half a frank/incense stick.
there be pics of niggas, now dead, that I loved
sprinkled in to give volume and color to my
memorial.

what I know is morning
and having to wake, get up outta the bed,
pray to or curse the gods
on bended knee.
there is medicine to take
and three drenched T shirts
hanging over a computer chair
after last night's sweats.
I know that it is winter.

what I know is that, when lonely,
there is a telephone in my room
with ghettofabulous messages I can playback,
there are pics of ex-lovers,
there is Marley and MeShell and Malcolm
with poster-eyes watchin' over me,
and there are bookshelves that stand as evidence
of years of hard work.
there are diplomas hanging, other silly accolades,
chapters I have not yet found a book for.

what I know is that my bedroom
is a repository for sadness
there are things in boxes to forget about
silver rings, naive and cliché poetry, perversions
like this here disclosure will become.

on the other side of what I don't know
are certain things:
longings, missin' mama and baby-sis-enem.
there is grammatology and feminism and postwhateverism
that cut the umbilical cord,
there is lots of paper
and lots of pens that don't write no more
but still there . . . bleeding . . . like me.
so much of my blood has leaked.

on the other side of what I don't know
are wishes:
there are master tools I want to use to make
a dream home,
a den with a sofa, a bowl of butter popcorn.

there is a ceremony   in that place in my head
like in my bedroom in the morning.
I shall find a heart still beating
and shall dream up a heart to match
and a dance with him . . . to house music
we'll exchange silver cockrings,
and have 7-up cake at the ceremony.
I'll ignore some chile trying to read my dashiki.

the ceremony . . .
I imagine the family is "going in"
cause this time it's real:
mama's lil' boy
has claimed another lil' boy's smile
as his own   for keeps
and to add to the collage
of other things he knows
there is the kiss
we untying each other's tongues
forcing our jump to the center of the broomstick
'til it snaps.

heart-hurt
(for August)

I cannot bear the thought of you hurting
but more than this
I cannot bear the thought of you not
tossing and turning
from silhouette into the sweat-shadow
I left there
my last visit.

I love you deeply
and when I try to forget this
I find some remnant of your scent
tucked away underneath the
valley just below my nostrils.
Sometimes angry
haunted by your presence
I have tried to vomit out
traces of your saliva
stored in some porous palate
not letting me forget the sweet
of your tongue kiss,
the texture of your bottom lip,
or the tone and push of your whisper
calling my name.

I have wanted to pretend
that this hurt does not hurt
as much as it do
that my heart don't sink down
beat slow, then fast and interrupt
rhythms we danced acting silly
or making love
I have hated my eyes for revealing
the truth of my longing
and my niggas   lately they been asking
what's wrong
even after I've practiced fake smiles
in foggy mirrors after showers
that bring your ghost back
my lips tasting the steam offa your neck-back

the salt of your skin
seasoning every kernel of air
I inhale in order to stay alive
missing you
hurting while trying to heal
wanting you in my life
but realizing that   now
shit ain't working
mad at myself for no longer wanting to
endure the struggle of days   you
absent except for phone calls
and memories that exhausted me
digging them up . . .
they emerge faded like old pictures
all the more sentimental
but more distant and faded.

hoping that your wounds
will reserve a place
for my tongue to lick and heal
. . . and that and time and some space
and you knowing that I love you
anyway
is what will save us
you   me
our
heart-hurt.

iffection
(for calvin)

between infection and affection
there is the utter unfairness of over-contemplating
deep kisses,
somebody's rejection of not just your truth,
but your essence, your positive spirit.
There is the soft brown flesh around you
strugglin' against obsessions with guilt, disclosure,
and the dirty you are sometimes made to feel
for loving this way.
There is the battle waged in the body,
but a gym membership and good looks
to mask it.
There are guilty erections.

Lovemaking shouldn't be so psychological.
There is evidence that it is still ecstatic, magical,
sticky-sweet, carefree, sexy
and that the right kind of baritone
gets you hard.

There are strong arms to hold some body with
and a beautiful boy before you . . .
but tonight, you need to be held.
And though your heart knows no ill-intent,
it fails sometimes to beat on-beat,
and skips
becomes insecure, volatile, loses its rhythm . . .
especially when it senses another heart
across a crowded smoky bar
with an intense gaze to match your own.

At such a juncture, there is often the seductive fantasy
that there is no infection
just you and he and your reciprocal affection:
knowing his soul, opening your own
trusting the safety of condoms and intents.

sweatin'

ignoring night-sweats
when it's not even hot out
when the cold is barely cool
mocks the crying pores
and taunt the body that
wants to be held;
the body so moist
that it slips out of any well-meaning arms
rejecting care   and
throwing off favorite childhood blankets
turning soft-lite sheets into AIDS quilts.
with each acid sweat drop
adding to the burden
and heaviness of the way the body
reminds blakkboys that this crisis
ain't just psychological.
but ignoring that shit
and sleeping nakedcool
on top of sheets
letting the Bay breeze
be lover.

so some niggas
tortured enough by a guilt
they don't believe in
rather than regressing
and thinking
they can love they self
by hating what they was
and admitting they done loved wrong
decide only to remember that they loved
not thinking of consequences
not thinking about tomorrow
just remembering looking into deep dark eyes
and caressing mochabrown skin
and giggling or moaning at the tingle
before the touch
or savoring the look in the eyes before the kiss.
and wondering what god in heaven would permit
such pain to come from such sweetness.

so some niggas defer sadness
and leave it to the body cope with
the fears and pessimism and moodswings.
and we wake up to double doses of
unpronounceable and toxic lifesavers,
exercise and eat smart and feel good enough
to look handsome
and catch the cute boy's eye
who might gag at the truth of
why we lookin' better these days.
scared to say more than the blush or wink
'cause it be safer to dream him into the sweetness
that conjured up the first nightsweat
the good kind   before we overcontemplated
coughs and blisters and lil itches.
we push ourselves to remember the beauty of sweatdrops
that get favorite childhood blankets
thrown off onto the floor
and make the body so wet that it
slips right into well-meaning care
and with each limb-locked nectar drip
and with each over-anxious sip-kiss
remember that there is so much good
'bout the way we make love with each other
so much
that the next nightsweat reminds
not of three or four letter dis/ease acronyms
but of two and five
and four and seven letter niggabeauties:
chris and tony and darrell
and derrick and ed and michael
and dante and rodney and frank
and baby and boo and lover
and my boy and my nigga
that come to this here place
to sweat with lonely niggas in
this here healing pool
that sometime be the only safe place
we have that love us
right here under these here wet covers
sweatin'

Litany for Survival
(for Melvin Dixon)

What's a blakkboy to do
when his spirit is luring him to write
when there are words stuck in the throat
that accumulate and choke
when there is a poem to write
but a migraine and loneliness
locking the body to the bed?

What happens when
alphabets distract,
pens bleed,
and his sweaty fingers
are too thick for the keyboard?

What happens when he is afraid
of what he might write
and cannot seem to remember
what he will conveniently forget?

What's a nigga to do
with vivid memories
but partial names?
with unforgiving poems
that haven't been written
'cause tears well up in the eyes
don't fall,
and blur his vision?

His third eye is remembering
that he dosed off before dosing up
and he is frightened because a friend's sickness
foreshadows his dying.
And he has not yet lived.

He cannot expect an embrace to save him
from his madness:
the uneventful coming of
nightsweats or nausea or panic attacks.
He must hug and kiss
and rock himself to sleep.

He must read Baraka and Foucault and Genet
until his eyes are so blood-red
that he imagines roses in the margins
and the page flip, a fingertip caress
and the crease, a repository for secrets
he cannot even tell himself.

He cannot expect anyone to decipher
his suicide journals.
they are rendered invisible and exaggerated
'cause he is still breathing heavy
and is so "blessed" to be alive.

He cannot be held
for fear of being possessed
pigeonholed, "figured out"
by some well-intentioned savior
some mortal's conditional care
and frustrated departure.

He is tired of longing.
He is tired of dis/ease.
He is tired of being brave and super-strong;
tired of being a man.
He has never been a child.

When he is trying to schedule the next dose
when he is counting on the next hug or smile
to redeem past indiscretions
he will call upon a ghost, an invisible witchdoctor
an herbal remedy, or somebody's phone call
to lullaby him to sleep.

What's a blakkboy nigga to do
when he has exhausted
the lexicon of feelings
and is left with only nostalgia
for the top of a blank page
some lead or ink and his/story to write?

What else is writing
if not evidence of his survival

Breath 5

Erotiks

quickie

they don't understand
when I say: "whassup nigga"
to you
after the beat down, fist pound
and soulpower handshake
combination hug/embrace.
elbow pointing out . . . Westside
one hand resting gently
on your thigh
sensing the heat it emanate
and the other hand
clutched and hidden
safe-like
from the crew, your boyz,
my cipher, the sistahs.

between baggy clothes
you find a way, find an excuse to
content yourself
with soft quick strokes
of my thumb.
it begs for more;
cries because the trace even
is inadequate and hurts so good.
I press against you in a small close way
cause I understand
your small brave caress
as continuation
of butterflies felt
when your eyes met mine
and you saw underneath the pain in me
even across the multitudes.

we speak through gestures
and codes that ask each other
for forgiveness
for not being braver.
I would kiss you softly
had I more courage.

I would let my locks
clothe your shoulders
instead of the quick release
push   pull   push   pull   push.
this tension is so bittersweet.

there is the brush and warmth
of your breath-whisper
and so I open my mouth
imperceptibly for a taste.
it is Sade's kiss of life
singing
"ahhh ahhh ahhh ahhh"
'cause there are no words
for that kind of joy.

why is even our shame
so silent?
why is there even shame
in the same place
where I love you so deep?
why does our love
frighten them
more than it frightens us?

sometime I wonder
how them folk don't perceive
my feelings when they
all pushed outward at you;
flowing out pores as spirit,
joy-leaping and glowing all love-like.
and sometime I think
that even our subtlety
must be obvious.
can an honest love hide anyway?

naive as we once were
they do not know
that I also smell your scent
feel your heart beat too
our chest-bump is a grind
our whisper a deferral.

and they think that I just mean
that you my boy
when I say: "whassup nigga?"
my boy you are too, and then some.

we find ways to get so much in.
in seconds
the voices around us interrupt
our quiet calm.
in moments
that stretch longer than our love
whole and pleasant.

I remember to let go
without letting go.
"check you later boo"
you sound so low.
"ahhite love" I return.
the passion-fire still burns.

how such depth could
fill fifteen seconds
they'll never know. . .
that I love you
they could feel it
if they freed themselves
to read: "whassup nigga"
as a repetition of our vows.

when we release
we pray that the presence
will stay longer than the quick—
and make us bolder and braver
than we were today.
for we grow more tired
and discontented with the quickie
with each singsong of the heart.

Analytics[12]
(for James)

your analytics send me goo goo
remembering the sting of tart candies
pixie stick predilic.
get a rise from my deep dic
blakk genius overstands the push-up: kool and crisp
your rhytes sic, your analytics: proof you got gift

someday we'll soon chapter concrete heat
ghetto passions
'bout some southern crunk monkey waves
b-boy breaks for milk shakes
from cornea stores, peeped the kiddy I adored
brown trips on big wheels to downtown: memory clips
virtually claimed this big city just for you and me
shared an ashy knee scrape or two
with a brotha like you
but lost touch
first crush: pine-appley polite
revived, revisited, re-incarnated through your rhytes
could you be that same brown kid I use-ta fight?
'cause I like-ted him and he found out
and couldn't bear to deal my mouth, mouthin'
these three words,
articulation through baby browns, you never heard
ears enchanted by the boom-bap.
act: shun?
("traumatize" th' verb?)
it was the playground that
ritualized our first kiss
in a recess toe to toe fist-blow
bullying now transformed to self-acceptance
the pen and pad years later our weapons
camaraderie our blessin . . .
test question: intuitively knowed
where you rhyte, my eyes will surely go
did you know, diamonds were coals
under pressure?

---

12 "Analytics" was translated as a song that appears on West's solo debut *Songs from Red Dirt* (Cellular Records, 2004).

my rhytes fresher now
when amazed I engage
(now look at the mess you done made)
my styles more freestyle but still nostalgic 'bout "you"
who I knowed fore I first called you
moaned silent intercept baritone cats: you spat
cuz ya voice relaxed my shame
our worlds collide, mane.

love sick
(for David)

last night I dreamed of red-dirt boys
building clay castles
from the thick of sentiments.
28 years it has stood
towering over ants and pine needles:
a lost city
somewhere between Henderson and Bear Branch
where the sounds of blackness echo your essence.

knowing you before I met you
I drafted poem-passions marking my re-birth.
my tongue got untwisted in a quickie
beneath the slide of sweat between us:
foot shuffles underneath a jazzy house groove
where eye first found you.

your heartbeat still tainted with nostalgia
for the playmate you imagined as close a companion
as your shadow;
and his promise to adore your eyes
when you least notice.

there are four letter words
I've caressed into your skin
while you were deep-breathing.
and I dream us a future:
hard handed domino slaps across a soft table
and your smile at my own crooked pleasure.

My love sick imagination ain't sick
just bold.
savors the presence of the moment's intent:
friendship, vows,
a lifetime.

that's deep
(for August)

my nigga,
you ask how deep my heartstrings run?
dig with a toothpick to the core of the earth
and out . . . and through
and Chinamen will direct you
to the cave that keeps my prayer-shrine for us
dark and endless.

and when you've gone as far as you think is possible
I'll make a Shaft-style magical appearance:
black turtle neck, a beret-matted afro, a pair of your jeans
you said would warm and protect me 'til your arrival,
and the taste of your tongue-kiss
stored somewhere in my palate
four seasons long.

I'll float down Matrix-like
chest stuck-out-bold cause I'm
proud to love you . . . your favorite superhero,
even when I have been stoned for it.
I imagine that I would descend from the heavens. . .
ghettofabulous
and say:
"mothafucka...hurry up. . .
I been waitin' for your black ass
all my life. . .
and I'm ready to hold you for the rest of it."

I'll dust you off
lure you to
some floating carpet
to kiss away tears and sweat
and ask:
"can we go deeper still?"

asskisser

papa said never to kiss nobody's ass
but I have defied him before.
succumbing to urges
repressed   I confess
that it is boys and men I want to dance with,
foreplay with their shadows,
chase their scent with my own,
predict the intentions of
soft stares   chest hairs.   I swear
I'm knowing and glowing like love
and that's where it all starts.
so I part his innocence
I'm so into this.

he look and feel sweet to me.
I am a sometimes-I-feel-like-a-nut almond-joy boy
he, a chocolate dipped treat
I wanna eat   all over
especially his. . .   ask me
next verse
If I've grown more comfortable with taboos
with the foreshadowing of papa's
"never kiss nobody's ass."
but back to him   that man
and his skin.

he smiles in a way that lures my tongue
gives it flow across feet-toes
like dirty-south clean laundry   hanging.
I lick my alphabet careful kindergarten-like
on the firm base of his thigh
I smell his heat, his want.
my papa . . . I have defied him before
so let go   that ghost
back to the boy
I want more.

there near the innie
there at umbilical center
a third eye looking back
at my tongue's own wetness

begging for its rain dance-drip
its careful kiss
don't ever wanna miss a spot
so drop   down and
flip with my strong-soft grip
his hip   rotate this mate this
man-o'-mine   so phyne
that his smile makes me forget
papa's warning
"never, never" he said.

and I now know that this symbolic kissing
of the derriere   is more than just a dare
is giving in not just to this man-beauty
I aim to please
but my own pleasure   and my own needs
and my own me   not papa's me.

I inhale the salt of his neck
and peck the pecks   I bet
this will be the sweetest stand
I'll ever take against the man I call papa.
so I please me   by kissing
an ass so beautiful
that it pushes my memory against any thoughts
that I might be as
nasty as this tender act
no longer me nor my identity
will I ever mask.

papa, papa   don't be mad
I did more than kiss that ass.
and it was good.

but me too papa
me too.

permission

(for Darryl)

my eardrum being invited to samba with your heartbeat.
and fingers finding the kitchen: my nap
the reverb of baritones harmonizing
rolling into each other, and okay with staying
Sarah Vaughn resurrected
and crooning the moment's apprehension.
limb locked intricacies—our bodies a jigsaw
ecstatic for having found matching pieces.
repetition without redundancy.
smiles and glances that catch each other blushing.
vulnerability that don't feel vulnerable
just strong like our backs and arms
heavy like your eyes or my night breathing
or our blackness harnessing a house beat.
opening up to desire and trust.
the vast potentialities of friendship
and then some.
missing enough to return
a call, an instant message, a trip.

permission validates that it's OK to tingle inside
and for the fingers to be guided
to write more songs than rhymes these days.
thick like the only way my eyes know to look at you.
humid like kisses deferred for a more tender moment.
traces of each other: music exchanges, pillows.
and some songs will never sound the same
imbued with new meaning now.
memories that refuse to leave: impressions.
and smiling because there's another reason to.
my eardrum remembers
the rhythm of your heartbeat
and follows that drum.

permission.

moments

glance
       chest
              candle
                    pant
                          "damn boy"
gaze
       hardness
              light-flicker
                    sweat
                          "you like that?"
kiss
       wet
              blackbody
                    browneyes
                        smile

"you do."

poemtomakeyoubelieveibelieve
(for Gregory)

drawn to damp places
drawn to both marsh and tide
I've carried you up the hill on my back
because you dared me to,
cuz you said I was a crazy nigga for doing so,
and cuz I love it when you laugh.

insisting on the fantasy of you here
I've taken your hand
oblivious to staring passersby
to a cliff's edge
where we perform our first ritual:
your elbows folded under my arm pits,
hands warmed by my chest,
a bold shoulder that supports your chin,
and my half turn back to receive your lips
and you . . . and us
what became ours
the moment our hearts claimed it.
like the tide before us that builds
and breaks and crashes
is ours
and the way the rhythmic waves
beckon this full moon
is just for us
silently crooning us a love ballad.

it and we are right if only because
it is destined to be so.
like your fingers find their way
out of the undercurl of one nap
to another.

if unafraid and vulnerable,
like the tide not fighting its destination
here
bubbling by our feet
for its last breath
there will be infinite rituals

one for each day
I open my heart
releasing the heaviness
of this fantasy
for something perhaps real
a Valentine anticipating next year,
family gatherings,
anniversaries,
our favorite song.

smooth talk
(for Marineke)

imagination projects
play pens writing nothing but dreams,
overstated millennium marketplaces
bartering souls on ice.

there is a Black Boy and his breath
(I sense it)
warming more than cold shoulders turned at Oxford:
ink and C drives.
never wanting the Native Sun
only wanting want.
so I reflect myself black to him and he me
rendering "we."

preferring salvation to despair
eye saw him running
gasping for saliva,
his spirit slipping between sweat beads.

wanting to save him with a ghetto "puncil"
I re-write black trajectories: a love ballad.

accepting that traumas are never redeemed
by free-flow red-dirt personified
I've screamed: "I am the River Niger"
inside of Giovanni's Room
vomiting up invisibility of men before me
rendered nothing more than
lacerations and jungle fights—
a spectacle entertaining privilege and luxury.

catapulting back
my memory prefers lovemaking sessions
to prize fighting nigga bouts

I time travel forward
to candlelight incense passions
frustrating white patriarchs and Uncle Toms:
one banji boy kisses another.

smooth talkin under a Sade croon
or a Lewis II riff
"we" overstand postpomo nigga smiles
lured by the reciprocity of intents.

templates of hem

foundational sightings
my body, a humm
                  ing
      bird
sighting its shadow/wobahs
for the first time
in a buDDing orkidd
and lured to the sweetness there.

possessed by the spirit
of narcissus,
my self-pleasuring
or the very anticipation of hem
grounds my ramblings.
hem is a template
for what I most like about
baritones or raw souls:
boundless, open, repositories for
all things dynamic, open,
humble and curious.

my desire for hem
collapses on words
dancing
      in my throat
on Sun days
stuck and
waiting for a moment
to massage the air,
his ears, his neck.
my eyes would say all
if they had permission
to return the gaze.
but my passion often hides
from potentialities
like niggas loving niggas.

hem is a cool and damp synergy
where earth meets cosmos
in the glances back and away
at each other's eyes:

silence, poetry
a graffiti collage
waiting to scream something
beautiful
like where dark palms
and fingertips meet.

remembering
that breathing is heaviest
between the inhale and exhale
in hem, I am reminded
of my nervousness—
how it rages
before and after
like the nebula trusting
the grace of goddesses.

the embrace of my pleasure
cushions any fear
that hem is afraid of
desire, a dream deferred,
a native son, me:
seeking his/story
tattooed on some other niggas back
waiting to be deciphered.

On Loving

on loving
I have little to say
beyond anticipations
of being loved
like this:

I have only known how to give
the thick kind of love.
it stumbles over itself
running too fast,
always boils over
finding pleasure in its excess
seduced by the fire next time.

mine is a love
that stubbornly desires
the ability to smile again.
and my shine is a diamond
nestled in the belly of ashes
awaiting a commitment ceremony:
kente cloth, *djembes*, brown people
and some other nigga
brave enough to love like I do
"till death do us part"
and I return to the earth
the way I was found
patient and enduring.

mine is a cocky love
knowing few limits.
reminded that it is easier to make love
than make love stick.
I have learned that loving hard
is the hardest kind of love to get over.
and that trying not to get hurt
gets you hurt anyway.

so I am learning
to celebrate the way my heart moves
and that my loving is like my breathing

as subtle as my toothy smile,
simple as my analytics,
courageous and inevitable.

I celebrate
that there's no other way to do it
than the way I've done it:
intense like my eyes try not to be,
forgiving like my memory of safety
outlasts the weight of longing or sadness.

my heart knows an endless depth
that echoes its favorite song.
my invitation
is a shadow that insists on
candlelight and a slow dance.
and my arms have held men
like they would break
without my softness.
my hands have caressed poetry
on the black hand side
while they've slept
hoping my impression
will be remembered
in the event they reject
the heaviness of my surrender.

my tears well
when I love myself enough to seek
what I have yet to experience:
the resolve one has
looking into the eyes of another
who has decided he will stay
and who knows
I ain't going nowhere.

on loving
I have little to say
beyond anticipations
of being loved
like
this.

Breath 6

Dis/Closeur

New Year Revolution
A ritual celebrating the Kwanzaa principle Kuumba

Accessories:

Spiritual Companion: Ayanna U'Dongo
Locs cultivated then relinquished in 2000
Nag Champa Incense burning
Sharaddha (Faith) Incense at Altar
Shanti (Peace) Incense at Altar
Suicide Journal: as a reminder of Triumph (read)
Shells: travel pieces
A Bowl of water to balance fire and earth and sky
Candle light only.
Soft Grooves:
Pat Methany's First Circle, Secret Story, Still Life Talking, We Live Here

Harmony Candle:

I will the energy contained within this candle to heal, harmonize and balance my being. Harmony now radiates through my mind, body and emotions. The magical flow now consumes my entire being. I am calm, relaxed and at peace. Universal harmony now becomes my constant companion. May light and love surround and protect me in all my endeavors. I will it so . . . So be it.

Revolutions:

I am reminded of where I was just a year ago: my heart happy and hopeful about new beginnings. 1999 was the year I discovered I was living with AIDS. 2000 was the year I not only discovered that I wanted to live, but committed myself to the good life. My spirit had to evacuate the secret box that had become my happy museum: replete with mirrors that distorted sadness to appear as smiles, a sensual shame box full of aging condoms, and poetry I had deemed bad because I wasn't brave enough to share it.

There on West Street, were pictures of kisses with the man I had hoped to claim as my life partner. That room is not so distant. Nor are the footpats of an emotionally congested roommate—replete with his bleach kit and the clash of Auntee's rebuke mail slid under the bedroom door. I celebrate being good enough to myself the following

April morning that I self-admitted to a psycho ward and made a few friends there. I did not want to live outside of living for someone. Love is everything and it's even better when there's the potentiality that it might boomerang back to you with the force coequal to your surrender. When August and Tim'm ended, I felt my spirit had ended also. But it was the idea of what we could be, together, that had ended. I had to realize that love can be redirected. I believe that love is karma and that I'm bound to get it back one of these days; better than I can now imagine is possible.

I celebrate the suicide journal that I wrote there in the hospital in April: a commitment to my eccentric spirit, to my dynamic eccentricity, to my passion and desire for love, music, lyric, nature, and all things erotic. And I ask for forgiveness from those whose presence I devalued in my aspiration for the knight: Corey, Ayanna, Bay, Louie, BJ, Juba, The Fam, Chad, Michael, the list is endless. I am immensely loved. I know that I am forgiven, because unconditional love is about grace; and I demand unconditional love through my generosity of it.

I was brave enough this year to let go of particular burdens: that sex was bad, that I was contagious, people with vast conditions attached to their love, that being a hopeless romantic was indeed hopeless, that a Ph.D. was an essential mark of my success. I learned that we sometimes win because we were brave enough to quit. I want to continue to be brave in this way. Brave enough to fall in love without the slightest indication of compatibility beyond my desire to make pottery from ashes. I want to believe more in magic and in my power to manifest my smile or a warm feeling inside.

I wish to continue living my life with integrity. This Fall I learned a dear lesson in Washington D.C. about integrity and its discontents. The costs to my spirit are far too great for me to hold lies in my heart . . . about feeling well when I feel crappy, smiling 'cause friends need verification of my peace. Peace is my quiet spirit burning slow like Shanti. This spirit smiles with the eyes just like my mama and her mama and Charlette. And sometime, it's just quiet and stoic looking. It's happier than it sometimes gives off; and always vulnerable, even when it plays with the illusion of control. And it loves to dance.

I want to embrace not always being in control. Inviting those spirits in my space who understand that the only conditions we control are our own. I can no longer afford to take on other people's shit.

I have to love my lil' brother J1 fiercely. He will be emancipated this year, because I am claiming and foreshadowing it. Every tattoo and workout and haircut mark a mutual ritual manifesting the love and happiness that is there for us to receive.

I have learned that just because someone doesn't return your love, doesn't mean that your love is invalid. In fact, unrequited love might be a testament of our own personal capacity to feel deeply without the condition that it be returned. Because, ultimately, it will be returned . . . ten times a hundred: a sunny day, a stranger's smile, a poetic calling, fellowship with friends, witnessing the tide on a rock, tasting the salt of my own tears, hearing my nephew laugh, my mother aging beautifully, hip hop revolutions I enact, and there is always some handsome black boy somewhere in some city thinking " . . . that Tim'm is one bad muhfuggah . . . damn I miss him."

2001 is the first year in our new millennium. And perhaps, more than last year, revolution is significant. I have remembered to call many of the people I love today . . . to tell them so, even if I forgot to say the actual words. There are going to be a lot of poems about falling in love this year, and about revolutions (political and personal and both), and about nature. I'm going to finish *Red Dirt Revival* this year. I'm going to move somewhere this year, if only because it's time. Could be anywhere from West Oakland to Miami. I will go there because I'm supposed to follow my heart and happiness. I am blessed to be committed to these things. And while it'd be a lie to say that my heart doesn't long a little to be cuddled by some blakkboy in L.A. or Houston or here or ATL or NYC . . . I have all the love I need here by this candle, with evidence of my triumph . . . with my undetectable viral load and 700 T cells. I have a lot of life ahead of me. This present joy I feel, albeit marked by tears either welling or streaming or stubbornly pushed down in the gut—that place where I know truth and where integrity of my spirit is at home—is mine to keep!

Breath 7

Still Breathing

Before Breathing:
(Unpublished) Preface from First Edition

if I could not speak out of my mouth
there would be color still
especially greens and blues.
there would be pale palms
pressed in red clay
sensing texture and cool and mud
brown like the black hand side
my impression left in the earth.
I would lick honeysuckles
'til they kissed me back
for my palate knows sweetness
much like my sixth sense
knows intent and desire
I would look beauty square in his eyes
'til he smiled me a love ballad
my belly would moan a jazz suite
cacophony blessed by angels
melodic sirens with full lips
blowing down tulips for sustenance
exhaling their soul food.

Writing has been like breathing. I will write for as long as I breathe. I am "called" to do so. Seldom does my writing occur on the page. It has been my experience that more often than not, my words are either too vulnerable or harsh to manage the impending inevitable consequences. So I am thankful for those who've manipulated me into recording—as best as I can—my laughter, blank stares, repressed tears, ego trips, blushing, the things especially that I had strategically masked inside of academic writing over the years.

I am most thankful for those who, moved by my writing, decided to tell me so. Sometimes amazed and other times perplexed by positive responses from friends—many of them writers who I have great respect for—I had resolved that writing needn't be this utterly self-indulgent and private activity. My journals are cliché. The metaphors I wish to use are often uncomfortable with even the conventions of poetry. So writing for me has always been about manipulating language.

Spell Check
(or a case for ebonics: destabilization of language)

words misspelled create semiotic dynamism interpellate movements
cuz all change is grounded in verbal slips. ghetto names stabilized
through Africanized apostrophes, eye patch enhances third eye glance
of periphery. do you see what I see? spell checks attempt to stabilize
language like Republicans wanna stagnate culture: poetic beef seized
upon by vultures, SLAMed by Black Nationalists reprimanding limp
wrist, preferring clenched fists. fags (re)appropriate the slur, no long-
er a diss/associative disidentification with the ten percent. statistics
underestimate the populace circumvent paranoia 'bout what's common
sense ability: attraction and predilection for affection for sexual integ-
rity... whatever makes my heart tick tock, b-boy down for hip hop's
metamorphosis untwisted in a tongue kiss. dic grip cuz words in Ox-
ford stripped of their inevitable alterity, ebonic words emerge cracked
up like M. Berry (still victorious). exclamation in a cuss, cuz niggas
done crunk out ill vocab down south, where aboriginal, indigenous
mixtures revolutionize sassy mouths. shift the culture, slang dictionar-
ies validate the utterances once thought mistakes, flash so fast
linguists do double takes. the colonizers tongue run amok, by Lakers
with high socks, stylistic errors made hip shit. kinship without relation
yet you my "brotha" and my "son" and my "cousin," grammatology
sparked in "the dozens." illusory order refused... so let words slip, let
them form concepts anew, bend words backasswards spark a linguistic
coup...cuz sticks and stones may break my bones but words can hurt
me too! fairy tales paint lil blakk boys blue!

A queer blakkboy I knew that I would never find my voice inside of
conventional discourse. So I was drawn to philosophical writing—
dense with words and ideas that turn on themselves. I was attracted to
literature rich with imagination but not disillusioned with the safe
boundaries between fiction and non-fiction. I discovered my own
voice somewhere between the ebonic ramblings of red-dirt southern
church "chilren" and the escapist existentialism and political writing I
was very early drawn to. I was drawn to poetry—to words thick with
sensuality and softness, especially when the subject matter was not.

As a child, words for me were like swords—double edged ones that had as much power to kill as to protect. For too long I had been afraid of who this book would alienate. Worse than waiting to exhale, I had become completely suffocated. So both my writing and my breathing suffered as a result.

I had to understand that categories do a great deal of injustice to those of us who defy categorization. I am not an ideal scholar or an ideal poet. Neither am I an ideal emcee or Slam poet. I am an idealist. And I do *rhyte*.

Rhyting is that spiritual compulsion to scribble sensibility onto the page—a sensibility that comes out of a life-force (a breath) that is necessarily both political and erotik. It also, phonetically, suggests a semblance to rites; a ritualistic commitment to the practice of expression as a *rhyter*. My friend and playwright, Venus Opal Reese, helped me to understand this, through her writing and my "theorization" of her brave play "Redemption." I've resisted rationalizing why erotiks and politics guide so much of my writing (e.g., politics and erotiks are indigenous as are my sense for justice and desire). Explaining this is Lyotard's *differend*: some things escape explainability. And where this happens, poetry finds a womb in which to be born. "You ain't gotta prove nothing to nobody but God," my grandmother would say.

This "breath" that will carry you through *Red Dirt Revival* has many different tongues. Trying to explain the schism between rural and urban cultures, ebonic and philosophical voices has meant holding my breath. That is no longer an option.

I reference being blakk often in this book; a radicalized expansion of a Blackness defined on its own terms, rather than as reactionary to an elusive if hegemonic whiteness. Essentially, *Red Dirt Revival* is this really eclectic window into the life of a blakk church boy raised in Taylor, Arkansas, who grew up to recognize certain fictions. Among them was that "airing dirty laundry" was something Black folk did not do. Why? I never fully understood. Seeing the vicious cycles of death and dis/ease before me daily, I had to be faced with my own mortality in a real way before I really came to understand how terribly haunting and dysfunctional this tradition is for black folk.

Red Dirt Revival is both a dis/closeur and a veiling at the same time. I am clear that the words that we choose to speak and the stories we choose to share ultimately take precedence over those we've conveniently forgotten or have not mustered the courage to share. This book is not an easy read, as it wasn't an easy *rhyte*. But I hope that some of the pieces here will evoke as much emotion for you as they do for me. I am proud that I have chosen to share experiences here that many men, in particular, have not been brave enough to write about.

I still keep lots of things secret. So if this text seems like a hyper-emotional rollercoaster into the world of a *rhyter*, overstand, it's not that deep. During this process, I had recovered enough writing for several collections, so the greatest chore was deciding what to leave out. The title of this book is a way I pay homage not just to ancestors who wrote in other languages on other shores, but the simple people in the simple places where I come from: the boondocks, hole in the wall clubs where *blakk* boys long for a dance and each other, a woman's womb, urban Hip-Hop ciphers, the coffee shop tables where my pen flows with the urgency of a man believing there is not much time left.

Revival describes the spiritual core of these writings and also the process of having been born again (which I do so continuously). My ideas in essays are intentionally tentative and therefore not preachy. I know nothing except that I know nothing. I am eager to grow beyond what my memory and imagination project onto these pages; so at some point I had to share as my way of sharing with others how I've attempted to make sense of the world at various junctures. It was also time to let go of the burden of not knowing.

If you are left with more questions than answers after reading *Red Dirt Revival* then join the club. I am, admittedly its most frustrated member. But I write this also as my way of joining a community of *rhyters* who share from a deeply spiritual space that only bravery and courage could help generate.

I thank you for your curiosity and courage to read. I also encourage you to find or rediscover your own"revival"—be it located in red-dirt, urban jungles, college dormitory rooms, or somewhere outside of the places maps do not show: like Jacks Crossing, like front porches, like late nights and heavy heartbeating, like this very special moment that will change the moments to follow.

TTW
October 2, 2002

sixteen[13]

I knew the world would worry me
the day I turned sixteen
I had mastered sewing my shoelaces
had solved how to scribble into silences
with soft lead pencil
my mental was on some vegetarian kick
carnivorous shift
swift like bruce lee
so there'd be no meat for me
at least momentarily
just variable veggies cleansing
my insides from the choking
my heart kept doing
blood bouncing in the wrong directions
healthy, handsome, and corn-fed
I believed myself to be sick

sixteen is never supposed to be sweet . . .
for boys
just noise and Duboisean talented tenth vents
just repents for retorting what don't make sense
just sour tongues for all the hardened demands of
masculinity reprimands for male
just the foreshadowing of AWOL
AOL gendering hindering:
You've got MALE!

not yet a man
were they in the right that boys
had no rights to write
etch their truths and tears
into tree bark as art
have the sun, stars and horizon
be an audience
and sing sixteen 'til the sweat splashes sticky
like molasses
or like lotion commotion on ashy asses
the memory of sixteen
has always slipped from me

---

13 "sixteen" appears as spoken word music on the debut project *Songs from Red Dirt* (Cellular Records, 2004).

escaped any memory of suicidal consideration
and elbow shoves
to express boy to boy love
no sleepovers
like the girls celebrating sixteen
no congrats for the difference
a year can make
for a fifteen year old
feeling follicles of mustache
forced through the valley
just above the lip
that slips and says:
sixteen
too early
forgotten
nothing noteworthy
not for a boy
sixteen: skipped like a stale biscuit
sixteen: buried to begin life
a man
no option to shine like the son.

twenty-five[14]

by twenty-five the ages had flipped like lyrics
shouted and danced like holy spirits
my poetry escapes the ears of purists
some opened they third eye, started to hear it.

Neg-a-roe from red dirt
aesthetic in the clearance
section of a thrift shop.
he be. . .   pop-lockin' in my direction
further introspection led to a connection:
b-boy gazes on another b-boy
chats about black nationalism
evils of religion
we shatter Afro-traditions
thick fingers pull locs at the root
it's co-mutual, naturally musical

I'm twenty-five
and he untwisted all the years I missed
with a first kiss
we traverse blocks to the West 4th Stop.
first love, soul mate, or perhaps not
check mate at twenty-five
at pit stop on the way to never-never land
journey to being man or something like that. . .

between being black and staying black
is a lack you can only fill by being yourself
go to Club SHELTER for good health
spin within to dry tears on a dance floor
Stevie Wonder my *cherie amour*
open the door, the sun's up
twenty-five and done survived the buck buck
more than good luck things get unstuck
forgive the self for the fuck ups
and guess what?
you already 26
and things are lookin up.

---

14 "twenty-five" appears as spoken word music on the debut project *Songs from Red Dirt* (Cellular Records, 2004).

thirty[15]

I am thirty now. I am twenty-five plus five. I am praising the life in this fist I make around this pen. I rhyte because I breathe. . . and because I had stopped breathin', I write with a revitalized urgency: chaotic, sensual scribble or ramblings that mediate the men I have been and the ones I become. My breath had been like ghetto morning dew suffocatin' underneath concrete, waiting to be unearthed by tears or the volcanic echo of a scream deferred. My whisper became a flicker, became a flame, became an inferno consuming every impetus for a next breath, a next kiss, a next rhyme next time. Sensibility made little sense to me till I hardened my larynx to be my bell chime ringing a song of forgotten ancestors– somebody strugglin' to be nobody 'cause he felt it safer in the world that way: invisible man, native sun refusing to send rays to melanin hungry flesh, or tears awaiting their rainbow.

I am thirty now. I am twenty-five plus five. The page is my kingdom, for there my thoughts reside. One moment to the next they slip into each other. They are run-on sentences afraid of a period; are urgent like two seconds or eight inches can be the difference between life or death for bulletproof souls. Twenty-five years. . . older than five violations times five, I've learned to heal my own scars. A mixture of saliva, tears, and a whisper cools the broken places. A dream, and a desire to smile a little more, my prayer for the years to come.

---

15 "thirty" appears as spoken word music on the debut project *Songs from Red Dirt* (Cellular Records, 2004).

"you dancewrite wonderfully": Letters from Hélène Cixous

Backstory:

As a new student at The New School for Social Research in Fall 1996, I took a Feminist Theory course with Dr. Amala Levine called "Beyond Domination." After reading "Coming to Writing" by Hélène Cixous, I felt it would be an injustice to disengage the poetry in her text. The introduction to Cixous was, I suppose, an introduction to my current mantra: "Find the theory in the poetry and the poetry in the theory." I was working in Eugene Lang Admissions when a Parisian student by the name of Krystel Boula came in and we engaged in conversation about French writers. I mentioned casually that Hélène Cixous was among my greatest influences, to which she responded… "I know her." When I mentioned the paper I'd written in response to "Coming to Writing"—a document that rightly engaged the theory of difference and Otherness—but as a "Letter to Cixous" rather than as a standard paper, Krystel asked if I had a copy and promised to deliver it on my behalf. I thought little of it until I received this postcard in 1997:

Postcard postmarked 11.24.97

Dear Tim'm,
I know it's been a very long time since you heard from me, but as I promised you, I sent your work to Hélène Cixous last week (I completely forgot doing it!). See, I still remember you. Finally, I decided to stay in Paris and to quit my doctorate… But I wanted to thank you for the time and the help you gave me. I would be glad to hear how you are…
Sincerely yours,
Krystel

I received a letter from France, still in Brooklyn, postmarked 11.28.97. On the back of the envelope was Hélène Cixous' name and address. I was speechless and was somewhat afraid to open it. That I experience fear is significant when I read the following:

Dear Tim'm,
I have just received your letter to Cxs via Krystel Boula. And I must say I feel very thankful to you two, who have been unspeculating messengers of the deitys of poetry.

I have read your "letter" as a declaration of peace. And as, indeed, a non-agonistical fight (that must exist) foragainst, let us say, "hope". It is an act of receiving that you have achieved; others would call it an illustration of the Triumph of Life.

You have the gift, without a doubt, to signify. It is a fragile and power-ful means of liberation.

I don't know (I don't <u>know</u> anything actually, I only experience) "how rebel boychildren survive", I couldn't say for sure; fortunately I have met survivors, they are very dear to me, in an undefinable way. I ad-mire them (not many) and regard them as a kind of brotherdom. It is possible.

Is it true that fear is close to you? It seems to me you are fearless—at least you are not afraid of fear—

Did I find the good other? I probably invented Him or Her more than once. But then the dream or possibility of someone is already part of the coming. I have found answers in books, and it has taken time to find ... friends in reality. But then I was lucky in the beginning—as a small child. I had transparent and honest parents. They know no ha-tred. This was my inheritance.

I feel awed when I am in the USA, more and more so, recognizing the scenes you describe ("the whitefolk at the grocery stores") similar to those I was a hostage to, as a kid.

There is a crime roaming free in the United States, I know. (Not only <u>one</u> of course—a layer of sins against Humanity). I keep wondering about how it is going to end, and when. I won't probably be alive when "justice" will eventually triumph. But it is bound to happen. You are one of those peacewarriors Tim'm m –

I am glad you exist

Hélène Cixious

So I'm almost in tears again . . . just typing this. As a complement to the actual letter, I think it says so much. There were a few other ex-changes after.

Some seven years later, 01.14.04, the postmark of a letter she wrote after receiving my book, and suggesting that I get in touch with a scholar working on a Cixous index:

Very Dear Tim'm,
You've given me the Tim'mest joy with your book.

I am proud of you (—may I?). The strength, the inventiveness, the fun and subtlety, you dancewrite wonderfully. I am going to show your work to a friend of mine who creates in New York. Her name is Roni Horn. You may have heard—She is preparing a "Cix pax Index". I'm sure she will admire RdR!

Cincinnati is not nothing
Sinsin Singsin Signsin Sinderella?
Actually I've always earplayed with the Cincinnative theme.

Warmest thoughts,
Hélène Cixous

Keepin' It Real:
Disidentification and Its Discontents[16]

You and me, what does that mean?
Always, what does that mean?
Forever, what does that mean?
It means we'll manage, I'll master your language,
and in the meantime, I'll create my own.
                    —Tricky, *Pre-millennium Tension*

[I]n the diverse invitations to suspend artistic experimentation, there is
an identical call for order, a desire for unity, for identity, for security,
or popularity (in the sense of "finding a public"). Artists and writers
must be brought back into the bosom of the community, or at least, if
the latter is considered to be ill, they must be assigned the task of heal-
ing it.
                    —Jean-Francois Lyotard, *The Postmodern Condition*

Disidentification's Discontents

The Bay Area rap group Deep Dickollective[17] (of which I am a found-
ing member) came together with buckets on which to bang, a piano,
freestyle rhymes, and the daunting task of consoling a friend's post-
HIV crisis. I was that friend in crisis. Dis/ease with hip hop is not so
figurative these days. It is the performance I enact each time I step on
the stage and check the mic; it is the vantage point through which I
theorize my movements in hip hop culture as a black gay-identified
man.

The burgeoning hip hop subculture called "homo hop" is the inevitable
outgrowth of a tension between hip hop's greatest taboo and the figura-
tive dis/ease experienced by its "homiesexual" disciples. Homo hop
has an origin narrative of its own: romantic and revolutionary, just like
the origin narrative of hip hop, the global and cultural movement out
of which it was born. Some will come to say that the momentous year
was 1999. D/DC was founded on beats, rhymes, and the dis/ease of a
gay black man moved to self-treatment: making hip hop music with
his "niggaz." As black queer men we came together having accepted

---

16 "Keepin' it Real" was originally published in *Black Cultural Traffic: Crossroads in Global Performance and Popular Culture*,
co-edited by Harry J. Elam, Jr., and Kennell Jackson (University of Michigan Press, 2005).
17 http://sugartruck.tripod.com

the idea that there are few "safe" spaces in which to live, and therefore, claiming all space as salvageable for whichever ways it supports our breathing. During that first freestyle and spoken word session "check the breath" became not only a mantra marking our testimony to life beyond dis/ease, but also a declaration that hip hop would be our most viable pulpit for broadcasting resurrection.

The notion of revival connotes the spiritual proselytizing inherent in black gospel tradition, but at the turn of the twenty-first century, it was accompanied by break-beats and a beat-box. This time the "faggots" are not the silent choir members, deacons, or ushers assuming a compulsory silence after a pastor's rebuke of Sodom. This time we would be the ones "mic checking." In hip hop the person who "mic checks" tests the viability of the medium for communication. Nothing is voiced until the microphone is checked. Some will come to say that gay hip hop terrorists began seizing control over microphones in this new millennium. Others will praise us for doing so. What is certain is D/DC's focus on empowerment and agency—not obsession with marginalization or complaints without action—has ultimately spawned an empowered and visible community that has been referenced everywhere from the *New York Times* to *Newsweek*.

For members of my rap group, D/DC, there was no way around the hip hop culture that had been so central to our rites of passage into black manhood in America. The insults in hip hop music, uncomfortable and badgering to our gay identities as they have been, either become the tropes that make us cringe every other refrain, or the thing we merely manage or tolerate—finding neither identification nor counter-identification with hip hop culture. This tension, this in-betweenness mediating identification (e.g., assimilation) and counter-identification (e.g., defiance), is what José Muñoz calls *disidentification*. The disidentifying subject necessarily mediates an unhappy attachment to something often inextricable to his or her very sense of self. The queer's relationshiop to hip hop reflects increasing ground for divorce, even when there is love enough to justify "till death do us part." Like the ironic failure of some of our most liberal states to honor same-sex marriage in 2004, the inextricable bond between the "homiesexual" and his or her hip hop muse reflects a desire for something foreclosed and perhaps more treasured as a result. It is the ironic double bind of saing this marriage isn't working, because one so desperately wants it to work. It is queer rappers defending hip hop to gay activists who fail to see its complexity as art offering an array of social messages, many of them homophobic, but many not.

In the introduction to his book *Disidentifications: Queers of Color and the Performance of Politics*,[18] Muñoz takes off from Michael Pêcheux's theorization of the "good subject/bad subject" dichotomy in order to explain how disidentification is neither the enjoyment of nor the betrayal by majoritarian ideology. In Muñoz's summarization of Pêcheux's view, it is not as simple as the "good" subject identifying with the dominant ideology and the "bad subject" counter-identifying with it. There exists for Muñoz a third modality for mediating this tension.

> Disidentification is the third mode of dealing with dominant ideology, one that neither opts to assimilate within such a structure nor strictly oppose it; rather, disidentification is a strategy that works on and against dominant ideology.[19]

An opportunity for gays in hip hop culture opposed to the dichotomous "hate hip hop, or love it and hate yourself," this third modality of disidentification is the gay rapper's partial assimilation of hip hop ideology while she or he simultaneously works to *deconstruct* it. The gay subject in hip hop does not seek to *destroy* hip hop, as she or he relies upon it as part of his or her fundamental self-definition (e.g., B-boy, emcee, deejay, etc...). Disidentification is hip hop music as it flows in the very veins of New York City gay rapper *Cashun*,[20] who has enough dignity as a gay man to challenge the homophobia of a fundamental aspect of the culture in which he evolved, and yet who is one of its responsible and loyal disciples. Muñoz says of this strategy:

> Identifying with an object, person, lifestyle, history, political ideology, religious orientation, and so on, means also simultaneously and partially counteridentifying, as well as only partially identifying ... [Disidentification] resists an unproductive turn toward good dog/bad dog criticism and instead leads to an identification that is both mediated and immediate, a disidentification that enables politics.[21]

Black gay folk who live at the intersection of various hegemonies often find this practice of disidentification more seductive and enabling

---

18 José Esteban Muñoz, *Disidentifications: Queers of Color and the Performance of Politics* (Minneapolis: University of Minnesota Press, 1999).

19 Muñoz, Introduction, *Performing Disidentifications*, 1.

20 http://www.thegayrapper.com

21 Muñoz, 8.

than majority subjects. Even in black (and presumed heterosexual) or gay (and majority white) contexts, black queer subjects find that having a more tentative identification with larger groups is a more enabling and liberatory strategy for survival than those people who have everything to gain by identifying with more dominant ideologies.

Black queer rappers like Hanifah Walidah[22] hold the double-edged sword that has potential to both wound and defend them. Their disidentificatory relationship with hip hop—the practice of "making do" with a cultural medium that has been so central to their formation as black folk in America—is about the decision to manage dis/ease rather than live as invisible men and women and deny themselves the medium that most clearly brings them into view.

In 1999, faced with the news about a drop in my T cells and the anticipated harmful side-effects of life-saving toxins, I could have either chosen to die or struggle to live inside dis/ease. It is the analogous relationship between my dis/eased body and disidentification with hip hop that I wish to explore in this essay. "Keepin it Real," being true to oneself, is the colloquial point of reference for an analysis of how black queer bodies assimilate and deconstruct the choice medium for their creative expression. For D/DC, "checking the breath" signifies an allegiance to the metonymic microphone that will give voice to our experiences as both black men and queer men. "Checking the breath" also denotes that if we are to "keep it real" then we must "check" hip hop culture for its hypocritical marginalization and degradation of its queer sons and daughters.

Between Rocks and Hard Places: The Search for Community

I utilize two epigraphs in this essay to illustrate the tension between the stability one desires in a shifting and turbulent culture and the simultaneous enjoyment one finds in ambivalence—in a non-committal allegiance to the idea of stability. Without delving deeply into how this mediation or tension is a marker of our postmodernity, I think that both Tricky and Jean-François Lyotard offer statements that explicate the dis/ease, the disidentication, and tension I will explore throughout this essay. Tricky questions essential conceptual frameworks (e.g., Always, Forever, You and Me), only to resolve that mediating the dependence on such terms, and their very interrogation, requires a new language. Gay rappers disidentifying with the heteronormative condi-

---

22 http://www.trustlife.net

tions of the hip hop nation must often use the very premises intended to badger them.

Deep Dickollective re-contextualizes the popular "conscious" rapper Common's infamous gay-diss "In a circle of faggots, your name is mentioned" (from the album *Like Water for Chocolate*) such that it reappears as a badge of honor for "homiesexual" rappers. Recontextualized, the fag becomes not the butt of the joke, but rather the topic of conversation among his peers, his fellow "faggots." Interestingly, in Common's album following his fag disses, the fag morphs into his best friend, who in 2003 is receiving the sympathy and understanding of a man who has outgrown his homophobia. In hip hop, tension often is the impetus for change. Perhaps not surprisingly, many hip hop headz relish Common's older material, preferring the homophobic battle-rhyming B-boy to the self-aware ex-homophobe renouncing his ignorance.

"Premillennium tension" is, as Tricky might argue, expressed in other plays on hip hop lingo as well. It is moving beyond the intention of language to uncover new meanings. In one issue of the popular magazine *Hip Hop Connection*, London-based deejay Mister Maker, founder of the international hip hop site gayhiphop.com, relays an instance in which assimilating the terms of his objectification becomes the tool for both self-affirmation and a counter-diss to his Homo Hop haterz:

> I know some rappers who are "out" and it's for this reason they don't get anywhere with regards to recording and club spots. There is a deep-seated prejudice in our society that gay artists have to deal with. It's funny because I've played clubs and totally rocked the spot, and I wonder to myself would some of these people still by happy knowing that they are listening to a gay Hip Hop deejay? However, I have a good battle routine for people who know I'm gay and think faggot samples are funny. I use Cage's verse "Can you guess who the faggot deejay is?" Most people think I'm fooling until I scratch in the Simon Harris cut "It's me."[23]

While Tricky contemplates personal resistance to the discursive ideologies given, Lyotard discusses disidentification on the macrolevel, a significant topic since most of this essay will ponder the hip hop *na-*

23 Ellis, Nick. "Homo Hop," *Hip Hop Connection: The World's Original Rap Monthly*, September 2001, 40.

tion. Although the homiesexual plays with language and experiments with the terms made available to him by the larger culture, he still seeks some sense of unity or community. Even the enjoyment in disidentificatory practices by gay rappers is met with the drive for something analogous to the unification inherent to nation building. There is no enjoyment in the misery of hip hop's gay bashing by homiesexuals without spaces in which to share the feelings. In the case of Homo Hop, yes misery loves company... but is working to strategize a come-back.

This come-back, however, assimilates the character of its enemy in an ironic way. Gay hip hop artists, in vast and increasing numbers in 2004, now debate with each other about who is *best* "keepin' it real" or "representin'" as a gay rap artist. It should be a surprise to no one that there are queers even at the margins of the gay hip hop manifesto. How does the building of a new hip hop nation—one challenging the sexism and homophobia that has become so synonymous with main-stream rap music—avoid the same hegemonic policing that has kept gays marginalized for so long? Where the desire for free creative ex-pression (an essential element of hip hop's origins) and the boundaries created to keep the mic and breath "in check" collide, there is no easy answer; there are uncomfortable contradictions and the "making do" as best one can with the tools given.

Is It Really Real Though? A Nation without Borders

Does is make sense to refer to a hip hop nation? The task of nation building is clearer when the focal point is the nation-state—an entity defined by geographical, ethnic, cultural, or linguistic borders. But shift the conversation to the year 1999, and the term "nation" (as chal-lenging a term as it is to define) and bear witness to a generation of young people who are self-proclaimed members of the hip hop nation. These are b-boys who break dance, graffiti artists who "tag" with an urgency before their disappearance into the night, and deejays who reassert the musical past into our present through their mixing and scratching. Hip hop's origins in New York City by Black and Latino youth was Ralph Ellison's *Invisible Man* wailing for recognition over a four-by-four dub beat. These men were setting the record *straight* that they are not invisible men. If invisibility marks an emasculated space where men are powerless, then visibility marks a declarative Yes to the question: are we not men? Given the burden of invisibility, the struggle to voice black manhood, there is no tolerance for the black sissy.

Youth in hip hop culture today are much more diverse in their ethnic backgrounds and sex, but still negotiate their identities in a culture where the act of verifying one's "realness" compels an especially heteronormative gendered performance. The demands today as hip hop culture diversifies is that black youth "represent" and "keep it real". These are slogans indexing the increasing anxiety around authenticity as white boys and women and everybody else struggle for a taste of the American pie that is our hip hop culture. But is the real ever really "real"? The slogan "keep it real" itself articulates angst around the authenticity and stability of the real. The real must be perpetually managed and kept in check by those who want to secure hip hop's connection to "straight" black men who started hip hop. But the straightness of the men in early hip hop is questionable— though those vested with the authority to control hip hop's image would prefer that none of us believe this. One's approximation to "realness" (figuratively speaking) has less to do with which men get to call the shots than whether some individuals are even given a gun. When the ability or failure to "keep it real" determines one's access or exile from the hip hop nation, expect the kind of angst it has experienced going into the 21st Century. Also expect that so much of the angst in the hip hop nation around "realness" and authenticity would be regulated through gender performances.

The relationship between regulated gender performances and concepts of the hip hop nation are mediated through popular slogans. Among them is the demand that hip hop patriots "keep it real." As black youth in the United States approach the new millennium, how might scholars who study youth culture and performance account for the increasing proliferation and value accorded to the slogan, "keepin' it real?" Paradoxically, "keeping it real" is one's authentication of allegiance to a norm which seems to struggle against itself; realness is never proven for once and for all, but must be compulsively reconfirmed. Angst around authenticity exists because, ironically, the illusion of permanence must be stabilized over and again. Similar to the ways in which African-ness has often operated as an authenticating sign of blackness, "realness" becomes a crucial marker among black youth who embrace a hip hop aesthetic. A discursive trope among youth in hip hop culture, "keepin' it real" not only signifies a set of codes (performative and discursive) that authenticate ones identification with urban black culture, but also indicates that both the black nation or hip hop nation have similar processes through which its people are produced.

In *Race, Nation, Class: Ambiguous Identities* Étienne Balibar says:

> The fundamental problem is therefore to produce the people.
> More exactly, it is to make the people produce itself continual-
> ly as a national community. Or again, it is to produce the
> effect of unity by virtue of which people will appear, in every-
> one's eyes, as a people, that is, as the basis and origin of
> political power."[24]

This "problem" explains the performative unity that the hip hop nation must perpetually re-enact to ensure its stability. Through performative and discursive codes, youth in America and around the globe are interpellated as citizens of the nation through their appropriation of hip hop lingo, styles of dress, cultural, and political sensibilities.

Some of the most significant discourses on the subject of blackness occur through hip hop music and culture. Given its origins and its prominence in the black cultural landscape, it is clear that hip hop provides an imperative lens through which to examine blackness in the late 20th Century. Considering the rigid policing of gender that occurs in most instances of nation building, what connections might scholars draw between the cultural production of "straightness" and the stability of the hip hop nation? Specifically, how have the regulative practices of a heteronormative hip hop nation affected its queer constituency?

As hip hop culture has been compelled to shift in order to give expression to women and non-blacks, it is interesting that the homosexual becomes a figure indicating the proverbial death of hip hop. The rallying call for "real" hip hop patriots to "stand up"[25] for hip hop articulates an angst in hip hop culture around authenticity. This rally attempts to resuscitate its origins as the politicized cry of urban underclass youth. The vast appropriations and evolutions in hip hop over the past three decades are, necessarily, responses to the insular hopes to keep hip hop music black people's music, to "keep it real." Because music indexes a culture of protest—the metonymic battle cry of urban black young men—non-blacks, women, and queers are often viewed as trespassers diluting hip hop's realness. In the opinion of many black nationalist hip hoppers, we can blame feminism and queers for the di-

---

24 Étienne Balibar, in *Race, Nation, Class: Ambiguous Identities*, by Étienne Balibar and Immanuel Wallerstein (New York: Verso, 1994), 93-94.

25 Jahmal Crawford's essay "Will You Stand Up for Hip Hop or Bend Over" will be thoroughly engaged later in this essay.

lution of hip hop's "real" elemental foundation. There are various dynamic examples of this slippage.

In 1999, Busta Rhymes dressed his hypermasculinity in skirts, silk pajamas, and Pippy Longstocking braided dreadlocks. Lauryn Hill rapped with a voice "harder" than many of her male counterparts. Missy "Misdemeanor" Elliot chanted a celebratory refrain "I'm a bitch" as if it were a black womyn's mantra. MeShell Ndegeocello crooned a blues song in a low and sexy timbre that aroused even straight-identified women. In 1999, RuPaul was not a real woman but looking as good as many and Erykah Badu had a secret pre-Afrocentric past hidden underneath her headwrap. Responding to these eccentric expressions hip hop's Afro-centric nationalists were nostalgically starving for a time when girls were girls, boys were boys, and black folk could keep the lid on the gumbo that is our hip hop nation.

Today there exists this tension between those who enjoy the shifting, erratic openness hip hop is experiencing and those who like their gumbo traditional—without all the extra pizzazz and especially the sugar. The hip hop nation senses its crisis and the burden of proof for the hip hop nation's security is encapsulated in the nation's mantra: "keepin' it real." Terrified that hip hop will become a virtual beat into which anyone could breakdance, hip hop's national guard becomes more watchful of its borders. Guarding one's territory is the duty and honor of every good soldier. Hip hop's soldiers are those given voice over the airwaves and hip hop halls to continue the ministry. And if homiesexuals at the site "phatfamily.org" are noting what these ministers are saying, it's clear that there's no place for "faggots" when emcees break bread at the hip hop table:

> Though I can freak, fly, flow, fuck up a faggot
> Don't understand their ways, I ain't down with gays
> —Brand Nubian, from *Punks Jump Up To Get Beat Down*

> She took her panties down and the bitch had a dick
> I had to put the gat to his legs, all the way up his skirt
> Cuz this is one faggot that I had to hurt
> —Eazy-E, from *Nobody Move*

Man to man, I don't know how they did it
From what I know the parts don't fit (Aw shit!)
—Public Enemy, from *Meet the G That Killed Me*[26]

Hip Hop Connection writer Nick Ellis echoes this disdain for gays in hip hop when in their September 2001 issue he writes, "As a genre, Hip Hop has profited on being homophobic."[27] The soldiers "keepin' it real" have spoken, the battle lines have been clearly drawn and the new millennium marks the last stand for hip hop in the minds of those for whom Homo Hop is antithetical to the very fabric of hip hop culture.

Perhaps the better question is not who is keepin' it real, but who gets to define realness? What discourses, which aesthetics come to predominate any attempts to reclaim some sense of an enduring "real" blackness. Indeed the very interrogations around realness indicate that aspirations to exhibit "real" blackness are nothing more than the perpetual iterations of an impossible stability. That youth must *keep* it real underscores the instability of postmodern hip-hop aesthetics. "Realness" is always threatened by the inevitability of time and change, and therefore hip hop enthusiasts must perpetually safeguard the limits of toleration. Each moment there is some new attempt to authenticate some new standard of "real" black heteronormativity, to expose fakes: endless numbers of persons who do not portray "the real" in the right way. The problem is that the right way usually translates into the "straight and narrow" way; and with the *turn* of the century, the anxiety in the hip hop nation about authenticity is understandable.

Premillennium Tension In the Hip Hop Nation

Is anything "real" in hip hop anymore? Perhaps nothing has ever been real. A postmodern hip hop aesthetics is Jameson's notion of nostalgia without memory that manifests when a deejay samples an oldie outside of his or her experiential frame of reference, it is the ironic subversive potentiality of anti-capitalist lyrics proliferating across MTV or going triple platinum, it is the suspicion of a gay rapper, more "hardcore" than all others, his same-sex desire guised under a per-

---

26 The "Diss List" is a list managed by members of Phat Family—a gay hip hop listserve. Members of this site regularly contribute additions to the growing list of homophobic lyrics. These were among three of many examples I use to illustrate the normalization of verbal bashing of gays in hip hop music. That the lyrics come from among the more popular and famous songs by respective artists seems to clarify who the hip hop police are.

27 Ellis, "Homo Hop," 41.

formative cloak of hypermasculinity. Going into the new millenium, it is not uncommon to see a white boy with dreadlocks or a black woman with an Afrocentric headwrap and blue contact lenses to match. Lauryn Hill's video for "That Thing" juxtaposes a sixties and premillennium bohemian black aesthetic; the song itself is a blending of do-wop and a deejay scratch. Musically, a postmodern hip-hop aesthetics might be thought of as the diasporic fusion of soul genres that have fashioned the hip hop influenced "trip-hop" music or "jungle" music.

Premillennium tension is Tricky—the Afro-Brit godfather of trip-hop venting a southern blues guitar sample with techo-industrial clamor at his New Jersey studio. It is black "girls in the hood" referring to his "Vent" as "white-boy music." The implication is that Tricky is not "keepin' it real." The conflation of his music with whiteness serves to blackball him as a race traitor—one who is not in the service of promoting the agenda of the hip hop nation. The cultural gate keepers are not necessarily hip hop artists who are anxious about infiltration, but any enthusiast that is interested in transferring racial, sexual or gender anxiety onto the hip hop landscape. It is easier to point a finger at hip hop for its unique brand of intolerance for gays. Much more difficult to tackle the homophobic culture grounding the seeds in which fear and intolerance grow. In this new millennium there seems to be a final call to resuscitate the hip hop nation's agenda. Which is what, one might ask? And therein lies the problem. There has never been an agenda—just bodies with power and patriarchy and a big stick: hip hop police who will protect and serve their nation.

I have suggested that the anxiety around realness in hip hop is clearly related to the angst around black authenticity. The instability around black authenticity being so dynamic in the current environment, youth have an almost infinite range of ways they can express their blackness. There is the juxtaposition of a feminist Afro-matriarch aesthetic of Lauryn Hill or Erykah Badu to the high-fashion Jezebel seductress image of a Lil' Kim or Foxy Brown. There is the bohemian Nationalistic strain of Blackstar or The Roots that can be juxtaposed to the gangsta thug aesthetic of the late Tupac Shakur or a flashy producer/entrepreneur like Puff Daddy. But even these juxtapositions—ones that appear to assign a politicized consciousness around race and gender to natural hairstyles and conscious lyricism, while critiquing the latter for glamorizing the excesses of capitalism—represent a communal angst around authenticity in the hip hop nation. It is an anxiety that leads to the rigid policing of identity. On BET, MTV, and every urban radio station the most visible and vocal rap representative articulate this apprehension to the masses in their rebuke against "punks" and "sissies." That these kinds of slurs against gays inundate the airwaves without public censure is evidence enough that "keepin' it real" is keeping the facts straight. Hip hop history relies on the reiteration of a particular origin narrative in which "gay niggaz" like Deep Dickollective do not exist.

In the new millennium, as the range of African diasporic personalities explode the more stubborn boundaries of a seventies Black Arts movement or an eighties new black aesthetics, there is a deep sense of loss for that which can never be recovered—a melancholia for authentic blackness that stubbornly recommends nostalgia as a cure. Black youth today are dreadlocking Afrocentrists, high fashion mafia mimics, self-proclaimed "bitches" and "niggas," "homiesexuals", and everything in between. "Keepin' it real" represents the clash between anti-identity multiculturalists who check "other" or "all" on ethnicity questionnaires and wannabe Black Panthers born twenty years too late. I sometimes find myself between these dichotomies struggling for the breath to voice both my marginality and investment in hip hop culture. It is this disidentificatory space that is indicative of what I've called premillennium tension. The current generation of hip hop enthusiasts is the first to shatter hip hop's narcissistic delusion with its presumed straight reflection.

Public Enemy front man Chuck D. refers regularly to the "hip hop nation" of which he is an integral member; and in the year 2000 a museum curated the exhibition of "Hip Hop Nation" at San Francisco's Yerba Buena Center for the Arts. A scholar of cultural theory who is thoroughly interested in the policing of "national" boundaries, I wish to draw a few parallels between how gender is managed in more finite nation-states and the more loosely constituted "community" of people unified by their relationship to hip hop music and culture. The point here is hardly to give verity to the notion that hip hop enthusiasts have a nationality, but rather to emphasize that the same heteronormative and sexist practices at work in the hip hop nation are active as well in most nation-states. The regulatory policing of gender continues to delimit which bodies in the nation are "real" citizens of the nation and exiles those not "keepin' it real."

About the historical relationship between the nation and its female subjects, Anne McClintock, in her provocative text *Imperial Leather: Race, Gender, and Sexuality in the Colonial Contest* writes:

All nations depend on powerful constructions of gender. Despite many nationalists' ideological investment in the idea of popular unity, nations have historically amounted to the sanctioned institutionalization of gender difference. No nation in the world gives women and men the same access to rights and resources of the nation-state.[28]

If we examine the marginalization of female bodies in early hip hop alongside the courageous entry of the women who dared to rap, deejay, and breakdance, we might notice a relationship between the visibility of women in the nation and their foreshadowing of sexually diverse members also seeking recognition, representation, and a share in the power to define the nation; even when this share in power is not equal.

Imagined Communities, Real Communities

Hip hop artist Lauryn Hill popularized a sentiment that "Everything is Everything" and that "what is meant to be will be." One response to such deterministic ambivalence has been a vehement nostalgia for a time when there was more simplicity and certainty about what was constitutive of black identity. While the unity and stability of either blackness or hip hop realness are largely imagined and illusory, there is a commitment by those concerned with the health of the nation to keep its national citizens in check. The politics of policing are therefore enacted and reinforced not just by national authorities but by citizens as well.[29] The irony of such cultural policing in the hip hop is that its "people" have never been as unified as the nostalgic imagination sometimes projects. Such is the case with most nation-states as well. There is the reactionary unification when a "threat" is posed to the nation. In the case of hip hop, many have mobilized on the basis of their fear of infiltration by white boys or women or faggots who do not belong there. Often, clarity around the constitution of the nation or community, imagined as their unity can sometimes be, is strengthened

---

28 Anne McClintock, *Imperial Leather: Race, Gender, and Sexuality in the Colonial Contest* (New York: Routledge, 1995), 353.

29 In their introduction to *Between Woman and Nation: Nationalisms, Transnational Feminisms, and the State*, ed. Caren Kaplan, Norma Alarcón, and Minoo Moallem (Durham, N.C.: Duke University Press, 1999), the editors note that "we have the never ending experience of nation making, through which the vulnerability of certain citizens, some of whom are often in question, can be mapped. Often these subjects stand on the edge of contradictory boundaries—equality and liberty, property and individual self-possession, and citizenship itself—the modern nation-state cannot resolve. In this sense of the process of nation making, we can agree with Benedict Anderson's notion of the "imagined community" as an unstable fiction whose desire must be continually posed and questioned" (6).

by the threat posed by perceived outsiders. Interestingly, people sometimes find it easier to say what they are not, than to clearly state what they are.

In *Imagined Communities*, Benedict Anderson suggests that the nation is imagined "because the members of even the smallest nation will never know most of their fellow-members, meet them, or even hear of them, yet in the minds of each lives the image of their communion."[30] This illusory communion or unity is a concept often seized upon by scholars who are in the practice of deconstructing and destabilizing hegemonies. Still, the flip side of such interrogations is often the lazy dismissal of the very "real" affect that gender policing has on women and queer people in the "nation." In fact, nation building is so often predicated on the notion that its citizens reproduce the ideas of heteronormativity and patriarchy crucial to its development.

White rapper Necro, in a *Hip Hop Connection* article in which he appears with machete in hand, sunglasses, and a scarf over his mouth, protests: "Who the fuck wants to hear a fag rap? It's bad enough these straight rappers sound like they're gay; do we really need real gay motherfuckers on the mic. That shit is wack."[31] The queer who challenges *Necro's* patriarchy might be considered a national threat and therefore rendered insubordinate or are altogether ignored. Perceived to be an internal enemy to the national project, gay rappers are relegated to the underground and margins. White rappers like Necro might be hip hop's most fervent anti-gay ministers, as his "diss" of gay rap not only fulfills the representation of hip hop as straight boy music but also placates the "real *Negro*" who would otherwise challenge white boy "realness."

I have suggested that while the nation might be "imagined" or "illusory," its affects are very real. People are exiled, ostracized, marginalized, and put to death because of *difference*, even (or perhaps, especially) in the imagined communities. Quite often invisibility, displacement, and expulsion are the impetus for emerging nationalisms, neonationalisms, counternationalisms. These are imagined communities born out of struggle and resistance to nationalist hegemony. They are self-proclaimed "homiesexuals" and "rap faggots" who in name and their celebratory reappropriation of hateful slurs, both redefine and shift the predominant culture and create their own illusory repository

---

30 Benedict Anderson, *Imagined Communities*, 2nd ed. (London: Verso, 1991), 6.
31 Ellis, "Homo Hop," 41.

147

for free expression.[32] Taking a second look at the work of José Muñoz, it becomes clear how marginal space can become a generative and lucrative space for the creation of communities provoked by in their struggle for representation. In *Performing Disidentifications*, Muñoz writes that "performance permits the spectator, often a queer who has been locked out of the halls of representation or rendered a static caricature there, to imagine a world where queer lives, politics, and possibilities are representable in their complexity."[33]

Queer rap artists are engaged in the simultaneous process of expanding the boundaries of hip hop imagination and fashioning a community of their own. Expulsion from the hip hop nation becomes a mixed blessing; the space of marginality a lucrative opportunity for not only inventive political praxis, but new communities unified by their love for hip hop culture and their refusal to be denied identification with the music. But is it counterproductive or hypocritical to critique the policing of gender inside of communities and simultaneously celebrate the formation (and sustained energy) of a women's or queer hip hop community? I hope to illuminate, through narratives about the hip hop nation and its discontents, this elemental paradox.

Hip hop scholar Tricia Rose depicts hip hop as a space where youth are able to vent their marginality in an American culture where race and class oppression is elemental to the nation's development and prosperity. But if hip hop is summarized as a cultural resistance to white American hegemony, then policing is how its enthusiasts attempt to insulate its "realness". Yet while the counter-hegemonic cry of black urban youth is celebrated, there is very little interrogation of hip hop's own oppressive hegemony. In her groundbreaking text, *Black Noise: Rap Music and Black Culture in Contemporary America*, Rose states:

> Rap's stories continue to articulate the shifting terms of black marginality in contemporary American culture. Even as they struggle with the tension between fame and rap's gravitational pull toward local urban narratives, for the most part, rappers

---

32 Given the impress hip-hop has had on culture internationally, the interventions lyrically and politically of five queer Negroes is bound to have ripple effects. Black queer rap group Deep Dickollective represents a "coming out" in hip-hop about what some of us have known for a long time: that any black cultural Renaissance needs fags. There is no cipher without the sissy–whether they appear as the abject reference of the insecure closet fagrapper or whether the fervor with which they approach lyricism, beatmaking, graffiti art, or breakin' has inspirations that have been cloaked in compulsory silence.
(http://www.deepdickollective.com/ddc.html).
33 Muñoz. 1.

continue to craft stories that represent the creative fantasies, perspectives, and experiences of racial marginality in America.[34]

But those bodies at the margins of the margins have their own battle cry. There is a way in which forms of nationalism born out of oppression fail to recognize their own capacity to oppress. I have talked about how the "opening up" of national boundaries is so often perceived as a threat to national stability. In hip hop, the multi-dimensionality of identity must be reducible to blackness and blackness alone (read: male and heterosexual) and other agendas are seen as threats to the utopian illusion of unanimity and sovereignty.

How do communities and nations—which by the account of scholars like Benedict Anderson are illusory and highly contingent states of unity—sustain themselves if not through a rigid policing of gendered bodies? Such a question hints of the "inescapable hegemony" that I have struggled with when theorizing gender and nationalism. Is it just a matter of choosing a kinder, gentler hegemony? Can one who claims to be counter-hegemonic ever embrace an imagined community and not also embrace the related policing that is essential for its self-definition? Is counter-hegemonic discourse itself illusory?

Even as the foundation of many forms of nationalisms is necessarily unstable, what remains consistent between communities and nations is the ongoing tension between those vested with the power to speak and those who not only challenge the people in power but who do so by adapting the very popular discourses that communicate national consciousness. Clearly the patriarchs maintain the luxury and power not only to remain seduced by the illusion of their hegemony, but also to affect people and policy through their illusion. However, those on the margins are by no means immobilized by the powers that be. If anything, they imagine their own communities and the potentialities for the representation of their "real."

Forced Entries, Ironic Identifications

In *Imagined Communities*, Benedict Anderson seizes upon the simultaneity of citizens reading the morning paper as a metonym for an imagined sense of national unity that might otherwise be referred to as

---

34 Tricia Rose, *Black Noise: Rap Music and Black Culture in Contemporary America* (Hanover, NH: Wesleyan University Press, 1994), 3.

a Nation. Though the imagination and popular media are conduits for the imagined sense of community to which Anderson refers, he does not undermine the very real political, social, and economic affect of even the most vivid imaginations. Empires rise and fall invested in the illusion of not only a shared constituency, but also a shared set of complementary beliefs. Consider that in 1999 the premillennium tension I have referenced describes the bubbling over of an unchecked and uncensored proliferation of identities once thought external to the hip hop empire. As the water is on the verge of boiling over, enter Eminem.

Imagine that around the United States the hip hop anthem is the repetitious "My name is…" song that became not only the introduction of Eminem (Slim Shady) but a space where hip hop realness was being exploited by a white body—and accepted as such. Eminem, unlike many of his white predecessors in hip hop was a talented and skilled emcee who hailed Detroit as his authenticating "hood." His rise from poor white inner city kid to stardom has much to do with the empathetic sensibility of an urban underclass able to overlook race as long as the white subject is keeping his real "real." To boot, Eminem is led by an entourage of successful black rappers and producers who confirm that he is the "real" Slim Shady (e.g. Dr. Dre, formerly of Niggas With Attitude). His expanded affiliation with 50 Cent and D12 are ongoing testaments to his associative authentication. The extension of "realness" to nonblacks reflects both the very openness that excited me about hip hop as a teenager in the 1980s. Seeing the Beastie Boys and 3rd Base, I felt that there was some possibility that hip hop would open up enough to accept my sexual difference. I had failed to consider that where either straightness or blackness stand trial before the hip hop jury, straightness is the enduring quality that will never be compromised.

Russel Potter, in his essay "L'Objet X: Performing Race,"[35] points to what Michael Eric Dyson calls the "anxiety of authenticity." This anxiety is heightened when the subjects entering hip hop "realness" are not black. In an attempt to problematize the parodic appropriations of "blackness" by artists like Eminem, Potter says:

---

35 Russell A. Potter, "L'Objet X: Performing Race in a Postmodern World," *Literature and Psychology* 41 (1995): 18.

> This [appropriation of blackness] reflects a sort of perverse romanticization of the racialized "Other," even as (and perhaps in part because) that Other is daily demonized via the media spectacle of the young, drug-dealing, gat-packing black male.[36]

This demonized black male whom we witness on television screens on glamorized shows like *Cops* and (ironically) HBO's Hollywood prison show "OZ" is never a homosexual. In fact, he hates homosexuals. Like the explosive dialogue about down-low behavior among black men who have sex with men but identify as straight, the self-hating homosexual proves that a man is not necessarily what he does. The rupture between behavior and self-identification overstates the abjectification of same-sex relationships, particularly among men of color in homosocial hip hop contexts.

It is not so ironic that the "My name is…" song that stormed the airwaves also boasts the cruelty and degradation of a "fag" teacher. Is this brand of fag-dissin fundamental to "real" hip hop? Perhaps Slim Shady is just an inner city kid venting his marginality, right? Keepin' it real in the hip hop nation is authenticated through not only one's sexual prowess and masculinity, but often through the degradation of women and especially "fags." While many women have been able to penetrate and influence hip hop, the worst insult in hip hop banter is to call an emcee or rapper a "fag"; and even women sharing their responsibility of keeping the hip hop nation "real" exhaust this insult. In one of the few challenges to heterosexism in *Black Noise*, Tricia Rose notes:

> In a number of raps by women, men who are being insulted are referred to as "fruity" or "punks," hinting at their possible homosexuality as a way to emasculate them. This sort of homophobia affirms oppressive standards of heterosexual masculinity and problematizes a simplistic reading of female rappers' sexual narratives.[37]

That the gender police in the hip hop nation are not just its partriarchs but women who have also internalized heteronormative standards of behavior, speaks volumes about the demands for reproduction and family inherent in Black Nationalism. In *Race, Nation and Class*,

---

36 Potter, 18.

37 Rose, *Black Noise*, 151.

Etienne Balibar elucidates the comfortable relationship between sexism and nationalism:

> That is why nationalism also has a secret affinity with sexism: not so much as a manifestation of the same authoritarian tradition but in so far as the inequality of sexual roles in conjugal love and child-rearing constitutes the anchoring point for the juridical, economic, educational and medical mediation of the state.[38]

The present-day conflation of queerness with whiteness denies the voice of black queer subjects who stand at the intersection of racial and sexual marginalization. In the eyes of those popularly believed to be hip hop's conscious sons and daughters, homosexuality is a white man's problem. There is the conjoined anxiety about racial authenticity and sexual normalcy that predominates many disses of "homiesexuals." Present-day proponents of Pan-Africanism, black nationalism, and Afrocentricity believe that blackness has become so many things that blacks lack the sense of unity or solidarity needed to ground social and political mobilizations against oppression. Hip hop shares this angst. Concerned, and perhaps rightly so, that an "everything is everything" sentiment is a privilege afforded only to a people who have not had their forms of artistic expression appropriated and exploited by the white capitalist patriarchal machine, there are some who argue that "realness" travels better light. That is, in this procession of a loosely defined blackness into the twenty-first century, what baggage gets left behind, what is indispensable, what can we afford to leave behind?

Jamarhl Crawford, a hip hop critic greatly influenced by the politics of black nationalism, argues that the gay infiltration into hip hop is the final straw for enthusiasts who want to protect the nation. In his controversial essay, "Will You Stand Up for Hip Hop or Bend Over?" he states:

> Wait a minute! [Homosexuals] crossed the line now!…until recently, Hip Hop had been safe, at least from all outward displays of frilliness… I overstand that every special interest group is clamoring to get a piece of Hip Hop pie (now that it's popular) but can we draw a line somewhere in Hip Hop… Can

---

38 Balibar. *Race, Nation, and Class*, 102.

Hip Hop handle a sexual revolution, especially a homosexual one?[39]

Crawford strategically deploys the language of combat—referring to the lines drawn, revolution, and safety as his rallying call for comrades to "stand up" for hip hop. Crawford, a black male, in his attempt to safeguard hip hop from queer infiltrators resuscitates Black nationalist rhetoric that exiles blacks who do not reproduce (both figuratively and sexually) the patriarchal order. He says in an email (dated May 17, 2001) to Juba Kalamka, a member of Deep Dickollective: "My problems with homosexuality begin at the fact that I believe it is dangerous for Black People in large groups to choose not to reproduce. Also it is not our heritage or culture, yet another habit shown to us by our good buddy the white man."[40] Crawford's original article is not just a pink alert publicizing his opinion on gays in hip hop, but he boldly hints of a violent curative for homosexual infiltration:

> I think the leap from backpackers to fudgepackers might be extreme. Gay Hip Hop sounds as crazy as gay reggae and the urban environments of Jamaica and America have bred Rudeboys and Homeboys who are very protective of their manhood. The boom bap ain't too far from the boom bye bye and for that reason, I believe that Hip Hop and reggae will be the toughest battlegrounds for homosexual intergrationists.

The threat of violence indexed by the controversial Buju Banton song "boom bye bye" in which Banton advocates and encourages the homocide of Jamaican "batty boys" or homosexuals, is Crawford's way of defending the hip hop turf. The cancellation of dance hall emcee Beenie Man's concerts in 2004 might be proof that more than just queers are protesting homophobia in hip hop.

Juba Kalamka (pointfivefag) and other members of Deep Dickollective mobilized not just to stand up against gatekeepers like Crawford, but in order to challenge the general illusion of heteronormativity in hip hop culture. The construction of the collective, Kalamka notes, is an attempt to escape the very hard and fast hegemony that ostracizes gay and bisexual men from hip hop culture:

---

39 Jamarl Crawford, "Will You Stand Up for Hip Hop or Bend Over?" *Elemental Magazine*, November 2000, http://www.elementalmag.com

40 Crawford, J., email to Juba Kalamka, dated May 17, 2001.

> We specifically called ourselves a collective because of what
> it implies in the greater cultural sense of a space for people to
> enter and exit based on their interests and needs rather than a
> "band" with a hard and fast membership.[41]

But the self-reflexive awareness of how hard and fast boundaries can
duplicate the hegemonic and oppressive structures that alienate is not a
solution to the problem of hegemony. Not everyone can be a member
of Deep Dickollective. We are a decidedly African-American queer
male hip hop collective whose lyricism is stepped in the challenges to
Black nationalist hip hop rhetoric. The reasons we have drawn the
lines as we have, respective to the desired participation of either
straight allies or non-blacks has everything to do with our own alle-
giances to idea that hip hop is fundamentally black music. To boot, as
black queer men many people consider "straight-acting" and who are
very Afrocentric in our aesthetic, our challenges to the hip hop nation
are taken more seriously than they would be if an effeminate white
guy were part of our performance. Such membership would feed into
the very conflation of queerness with whiteness that we want to chal-
lenge. Deep Dickollective is, otherwise, as open as we can be within
these boundaries. We perform regularly with a straight white deejay
whom we affectionately refer to as "Double Token" and have wel-
comed a black female-to-male transgendered person to our collective.
This does not exempt D/DC from particular conformities to the hip
hop nation. That there have not yet been effeminate gay black men in
our collective is something I ponder regularly. We continue to inter-
rogate and scrutinize the ways in which we duplicate the hegemonic
ousting of other black queer men. It is this kind of self-critical exami-
nation that I propose will save hip hop, not because its agents
(including D/DC) won't occasionally act irresponsibly, but because we
the artists, and especially our fans and enthusiasts, will demand that
we be not only more responsible, but inclusive as well.

I have attempted to elucidate the burden and blessing of
disidentificatory practice in hip hop among its queer constituency. It
is this same double edged sword that transgender rapper Katey Red
assumes when she "passes" as a codified black jezebel figure similar to
Trina. It is when homo thug rapper Young Harith declares that, "I
don't fuck around with simple ass people, the niggas I deal with be
bustin like Rhymes, Jump in the Ranger just to load up the clip and the

---

41 Juba Kalamka, email to Jamarhl Crawford, May 19, 2001.

9, and roll up to a spot where some haters talk shit." [42]Clearly the politics of disidentification generates a counter-Lordean[43] politic of having to rely on the master's tools in order to dismantle his house. This is the double bind that is the gay rapper's disidentification with hip hop.

Interviewed by the *Dallas Voice*, a gay paper interested in covering my August 2002 performance at a local record shop, I was asked to respond to the question of why I had invested so much energy in critiquing, writing about, and yet producing hip hop music; the perception being that hip hop hates homosexuals. Without seeing any direct connection to my theoretical work around the politics of disidentification, I made a statement that I later discovered echoes Lyotard's trajectory toward healing the communities in which we live. This path of identification, counteridentification, and the willing acceptance of a politics of disidentification presupposes the call for hip hop's sons and daughters to heal the nation suffering with dis/ease about homosexuality. Seizing upon my understanding of hip hop's origins, I stated:

> Hip hop was a form of black creative expression that was used to supplement the voice people weren't given in the inner city to convey their lives and experiences...I'm following in the same hip hop tradition of giving voice to issues and experiences that aren't being heard. So when people say there shouldn't be gay people in hip hop, I think that's contradicting hip hop's very origins.[44]

As the boundaries of hip hop continue to shift, from the inside and out, we might consider a sharper awareness how boundaries preserve "the real." "Keeping it real" might indicate one who is true to a multidimensionality of identity; one that is sensitive to gender, class, sexuality and other dimensions of identity. The challenge, or perhaps hope for loyalists to the hip hop nation is that it will continue to expand and shift—able to respect its origins in inner city black culture, but malleable enough to voice unanticipated identities that emerge on its landscape.

---

42 http://www.blakout.net/harith/lyrics.htm

43 Audre Lorde has a popular adage, "You cannot dismantle the master's house with the master's tools." It is possible that the disidentificatory performances that Muñoz refers to suggest something different—that it is indeed possible to use the master's tools to construct a different kind of house; or perhaps a shelter different than a house.

44 Mekado Murphy, "Rapper's Delight, Queer Emcee Tim'm leads the Homo Hop Revolution," *Dallas Voice*, 19. 14, (2 August 2002): 41.

Black Is . . . Black Ain't:
Policing the Boundaries of Blackness

Is Black Dead?

> Black is blue.
> Black is red.　　　　Black is tan.
> Black is light.　　　　Black can get you.
> Black will leave you alone.　　Black can get you over.
> Black can sit you down.　　Black can move you forward.
> Black can make you stumble around.
> 　　Black is so high.　　Black is so low.
> 　　Black can say yes.　　Black can say no.
> Black can be your best friend...be as cozy as the night
> Black can do you in...make you fuss, and cuss, and fight
> Black is Black.　　　　Black is Blue.
> Black is Bright.　　　　Black is You.
> 　　　—from Marlon Riggs' film *Black Is . . . Black Ain't*

Often the discourses around black identity reflect a politics of exclusion that more easily discerns what blackness "ain't" than what it is. The days of invoking an all-encompassing, monolithic black community are long-gone. While the African American community has never truly been monolithic, at times the inability for blacks to mobilize around politicized racial identities has had grave consequences. Early 21st-century black political organizations more effectively boycott the absence of black faces on CBS than address the backlash against Affirmative Action and its many ramifications. So has blackness, as a politically viable collective identity, died?

The late Marlon Riggs describes his documentary film *Black Is . . . Black Ain't* as a "personal journey through black identity." The title of the film proposes to survey an array of perspectives on the nature of black identity, what it is, as well as what it ain't. However, his audience is encouraged to read the juxtaposition of "black is" and "black ain't" as declarative though incompatible stances on the very feasibility of blackness. The poem I have cited in the epigraph—Riggs' cinematic polyvocal sermon on the obscure definition of blackness—queries whether blackness, given its many different significations, can be given a more precise definition. This ambivalence, at the level of language, is mirrored in the (often) intangible political and social constitution of what is referred to as the "black community."

Moving into the 21st Century, one could argue that, ironically, the tie that binds African Americans is a shared sense of loss of any such cohesive "black community." "United we stand, divided we fall" has been the mantra for many cultural nationalisms; and to those for whom black diversification translates into "divided," the reclamation of a definable black sensibility is crucial. While the black community is not synonymous with Black Nationalists, the notion of black collectivity being a fundamental aspect of political efficacy is a common assumption of both groups. As the descendants of Africans brought to America as slaves, black Americans' social, political, and economic ascension has often demanded that we speak with one voice. Former Vice President Al Gore championed the removal of the rebel flag from the South Carolina state house and promised to check racial police profiling because successful democratic candidates must "win the black vote." While the recognition of this power by non-blacks is a testament to its continued viability, there is dangerous outcome to "essentializing" race as such. While I recognize the value inherent in communities mobilized on the basis of race, sex, or sexuality, they are almost always doomed to rigid policing of dissenting voices that do not corroborate the majority (minority) opinion.

In *Black Is . . . Black Ain't*, Riggs seems to be articulating what I have referred to as the *tight* between the rock and the hard place. It is a site of ambivalence especially for queer black subjects. I have argued in my readings of Toni Morrison's *Beloved* that this *tight spot* is fundamental to understanding black American subjectivity. Asked to suppress his homosexual desire for an illusion of black collectivity or to aspire to a vehement individualism that has no regard for a shared black sensibility, Riggs chooses not to choose. He believes strongly that these two choices are not real options at all. But his dying body is the battleground, and time, the enemy. His conflict becomes the embodiment of a community that is politically challenged because the black unity police uphold a belief that queer identity is a threat to solidarity.

And yet any articulation suggesting that black is both everything and nothing carries postmodernist implications that are politically futile. Should the black community tolerate any and every black body attracted to the idea of a shared black sensibility? Are there not blacks who do not contribute to our collective prosperity? Who decides this? Certainly the idea of policing is not wholly unconstructive. We would be fooling ourselves to think that the black feminist and black misogynist, the black homophobe and the black HIV+ gay activist will all join

hands and sing politicized spirituals together. Yet if the lack of toler-
ance for a particular subgroup is fundamental to a group's identity
(e.g., the homophobe does not tolerate gays), then policing seems a
useful strategy. Would the black community choose to tolerate the gay
activist over the homophobic minister? The overwhelming perception
seems to be that the latter is more tolerable, which is unfortunate. In-
tolerance for identities grounded in intolerance is where I have
philosophically set the limits of toleration.

From "Negro" Civil Rights to Black Power some of the more crucial
intracultural conflicts are situated around the monopolization of "race
police" by advocates of black heteronormitive patriarchy. A subject
whose dis/ease is immanently tied to his marginalization by black cul-
tural police, Riggs wants to reconcile the shared sensibility that is
fundamental to black empowerment with a notion of community that
more sensitively embraces its "black sheep."

The task of intracultural reconciliation is perhaps more arduous than
policing certain black bodies out of the movement. Often it is easier
for the race police to marginalize the dissenting voices than to manage
their presence among the larger community. This tension is very com-
plicated. On one side of the divide are blacks who believe that there is
a direct relationship between intracultural toleration of difference and
the (perceived and actual) decline of black political power. On the oth-
er side of the divide there are blacks who, having experienced their
(un)fair share of marginalization by the larger black community, re-
treat to notions of blackness that are exceedingly tolerant of difference
but not very effective at affecting the policy decisions that will have
devastating effects on the black community. Is it a "no win, no win"
situation? Is a stifling hegemonic form of cultural nationalism that
suppresses intracultural difference better than a loosely-defined indeci-
sive community that privileges tolerance and personal freedom over
political efficacy?

Liberal toleration of intracultural diversity has led some Afrocentrists
and cultural nationalists to retreat to romantic ideas of the past under-
scored by nostalgia for "back when," be it early African civilization,
Civil Rights, or Black Power. There seems to be ambivalence or an
utter lack of interest in engaging the question of whether or not Afri-
can Americans maintain some sense of social and political unity while
respecting and acknowledging intracultural variation. But what might
the reinvigorated interest in generating a more determinate understand-
ing of blackness indicate about late 20th-century African American

identity? There is a metaphor that articulates the need for black political mobility and that summarizes the central conflict in this paper. Stanford historian Dr. Kennell Jackson once shared with me the sentiment among many black leaders that: "Black travels better light." While the metaphor implicitly encourages black political mobility, it also reproaches excess baggage that burdens the ride. The more urgent the political response, the more race-policing becomes necessary to identify excess. And if the privileged candidates for police are sexist and heterosexist, it becomes clear who will not be allowed to join the revolution.

I propose that the "burden" of blackness can be defined as those elements that have somehow become cultural signifiers of blackness but which do not seem to be moving the black community forward. This is especially the sentiment for proponents of Black nationalism, Afrocentrists, leaders in the black church, and probably most other social and political groups working towards the mobility of the black community. Keeping with the metaphor, that "black travels better light" raises a question of which baggage to throw off if the black community is to move bravely in the 21st century. Ask boyz in the hood or the black proletariat, the excess baggage might be "uppity" African-American politicians who have lost connection with their black constituencies and who no longer "keep it real." Ask the black church and the excess might be anything from black queers to gangsta rap artists.

Interestingly, black queers and gangsta rappers are two groups who themselves seldom see eye to eye. A gay man, Riggs quotes NWA's Ice Cube as having said "True niggers ain't faggots!" One ironically grasps that the statement is *not* meant to be a compliment to black homosexuals. The "faggot" and not the "nigger" is the butt of the insult; the ironic commingling of two traditionally pejorative terms grants to the racial slur a kind of discursive transcendance (i.e., nigger is a desired social position) while the term "faggot" maintains its signification as a socially abject position.

If we ask black feminists (or womanists) about the nature of blackness, they might contend that the old white boys club has been structurally duplicated within discursive and performative fields of black maleness. In black politics, there is an old black boys club. Black his/story acts upon black women, while black men get to be the agents, activists, heroes, and revolutionaries for blackness. bell hooks is especially sensitive to this idea of phallocentric blackness when she critiques the centrality of black masculinity in black political struggle: "The reclamation of the black race gets translated into 'It's a dick thing,' and if the black thing is really a dick thing is disguise, we're in serious trouble."[45]

If Black Power is essentially about the redemption of an emasculated identity then call it by its name: black-male Power. Why ask which baggage is excessive if the debate is taking place at the black boys club? This critique of the racial redemption as being executed by a "head nigga [read: male] in charge" corroborates centuries of black leadership and activism where the burden and responsibility of the race has been conceptualized as the black man's burden. For feminists, the excess baggage is sexist baggage. The black community is trying to heal itself while suppressing half of its members. And the black community cannot proceed into the 21st Century in good health if it continues to address race problems without addressing sexist and heterosexist symptoms.

There are countless other intracultural tensions that are exposed in Riggs' personal journey through black identity. His journey becomes an embodiment of the dis/ease in the black community. For many African Americans, black "use'ta be" but "ain't no more." In what has for so long been imagined as a strong and viable community, each individual complication of blackness represents a further decentering from what black is. Which begs the question... And yet the question is impossible to answer by way of an ontological discourse, as blackness as a cultural identification that is largely "phantasmatic" cannot be qualified by rules of Western rationality or logic.

Blackness as a cultural identity is often rooted in a psychoanalytic rendering of the phantasm, a term I will interpret for my purposes as a fantasy driven investment underlying actual and often well-grounded collective identities (i.e., the black community). For example, the African Diaspora and its traceable migrations come to mind as being less phantasmatic than the commonly referenced "black community." While Diasporic identifications can generally be traced to an aboriginal site, the idea of the "black community" might have vastly different (and even incompatible) meanings for different blacks based on their varied sentimental or politically-driven constructions of blackness. Unlike a basis for shared identity that has an ethnic, cultural, or geographic basis, the phantasmatic circumscription of a community is

---

45 Taken from an interview in Marlon Riggs' film, *Black Is . . . Black Ain't.*

generally grounded in defensible identity claims, yet integrates an imaginary construction of community in order to render the its borders of blackness more permeable, able to shift with the times. Benedict Anderson's foundational text, *Imagined Communities*,[46] explores the imaginary underpinnings of nationalism, and informs much of my theorizing about identificatory bonds between black Americans and Africans. There has never been a membership drive or census count towards certifying who precisely constitutes "the black community." Each "member" develops her own imaginative configuration. This idea of phantasmatic attachments is the basis for my hypothesis that black Americans' relationship to Africa fundamentally relies on the imaginative construction of an identificatory bond. Nostalgia fundamentally operates to stimulate and reinforce this bond between African Americans and Africans—one largely constructed in the imagination of the black American and which is often unrequited and nonreciprocal.

There is also a strain of Black studies that takes off from phantasmatic or imaginary identifications with Africa and attempts to more substantively ground this identification. Where activists, artists, religious leaders and some politicians might rely primarily on sentimental or emotional identificatory bonds, political scientists, historians, sociologists, and other intellectuals seem to ground these connections in social, historical, and cultural realities. This cultural understanding of blackness as verifiable supplements the phantasm, as if to suggest: "Yes, we have a sentimental connections with Africa...but there is also proof of this lineage!" Arjun Appadurai's notion of deterritorialization[47] is fundamental to this longing to ground identification in more than just sentiment. Ambivalently identified with the alienation and social injustice of a racist America, African American leaders work to shape a communal identification with Africa that can be shared with the black community at large. Tracing traditions from black antiquity is one such basis for the ontological basis for black identity; the African American holiday Kwanzaa is perhaps its exemplar.

---

46 Benedict Anderson, *Imagined Communities* (New York: Verso Publishing Company, 1983). Supplementing my argument about the imaginative or phantasmatic basis for community, Anderson writes, "the nation...is an imagined political community. It is imagined because the members of even the smallest nation will never know most of their fellow members, meet them, or even hear of them, yet in the minds of each lives the image of their communion" (6). I would argue that the black community functions, primarily, under an analogous imaginary construction.

47 Arjun Appadurai, *Modernity at Large* (Minneapolis: University of Minnesota Press, 1996). Appadurai suggests that the sense of placelessness suffered by deterritorialized peoples is mediated through their relationship to a diaspora. "...We may speak of diasporas of hope, diasporas of terror, and diasporas of despair. But in every case, these diasporas bring the force of the imagination, as both memory and desire, into the lives of many ordinary people..." (6).

This more ontological account of blackness is not a mere reversal of the phantasmatic strain. Rather, the two differ by the extent to which identification with Africa is foregrounded by phantasm or fact. For example, In *Black Is . . . Black Ain't*, Black Studies scholar Maulana Karenga says that "there is no decolonization process that doesn't involve (re)claiming the past." Yet Riggs brilliantly juxtaposes this sentiment with one by the activist and scholar Angela Davis who suggests that she does not confuse her donning of Kente cloth with her black identity. While Kente cloth and invoking African traditions are symbolic gestures representing cultural authenticity, they are not to be confused with blackness defined as the sentimental imprints of the struggle endured in America by African slaves.

It is worth querying how this negotiation between the ontological and phantasmatic basis for black identity is situated in the context of modernity or a notion of the postmodern. If blackness is dead, if there is no metanarrative for blackness, then black can be all of the things Riggs pronounces in the poetic sermon cited as my epigraph. However, many blacks view postmodern scholarship as the enemy of black collectivity—suggesting that in its obsession with deconstruction, it provides no practicable platform for black political activism.

The solution, for those who refuse a deconstructivist or postmodern modality of blackness, is a clearly demarcated, plain and simple kind of blackness. This romanticized blackness is generally located in the American South and reminds African Americans of a time when blacks were all just one happy family. But we were never just one happy black family. Further, this dreamy blackness is killing black people who come to represent what my colleague Venus Opal Reese has referred to as "ruptures in belonging." Riggs, a black gay man living with AIDS, is an embodiment of this break in belonging. Unfortunately, he pays a dear price for articulating this rupture: rejection and ostracization from a black family disillusioned by its own discriminating nostalgia. Blacks, not whites, are the most brutal police of black identity.

Because the collective black consciousness is psychologically internalized by members of the black community, black individuality is necessarily threatening to the collective consciousness. The Du Boisian double consciousness that I discuss in my theorization of the slogan "It's a Black Thing" is a self-policing consciousness. If collectivity is essential to the survival of the race—a theoretical staple of Afrocentrists like Molifi Asante—then the black individual must self-

162

police—suppress all identifications that are disruptive to collectivity. A self-declared black "faggot" living with AIDS, Marlon Riggs is dying because of this compulsory silence. *Black is . . . Black Ain't* is his rebel yell against a black collectivity that kills the spirit of the individual. There must be a way to preserve black collectivity without appealing to heterosexist diatribes like Asante's:

> Homosexuality is a deviation from Afrocentric thought because it makes the person evaluate his own physical needs above the teachings of national consciousness... While we must be sensitive to the human complexity of the problem...we must demonstrate a real antagonism toward those gays who are as unconscious as other people... Afrocentric relationships are based upon sensitive sharing in the context of what is best for the collective imperative for the people. All brothers who are homosexuals should know that they too can become committed to the collective will. It means the submergence of their own wills into the collective will of our people... The homosexual shall find the redemptive power of Afrocentricity to be the magnet which pulls him back to his center. (from Asante's seminal work, *Afrocentrity*)

Riggs presents a strong challenge to Afrocentric rhetoric that utilizes collectivity as an excuse to ridicule anything outside of heteronormative patriarchy. He positions his dying body as the symbolic deterioration of the black community. And it is not the lack of black collectivity that Riggs believes to be the problem. Rather it is the idea that non race-based identifications that some blacks appropriate (e.g., queer, feminist, Marxist, etc...) distract black unity. Riggs positions his one-hundred and ten pound wasting body as a sacrificial lamb for the collective good of his people. But he asks for something in return—for the headstrong policing of black identities to be checked, as it renders valuable members of the black community worthless and invisible.

A clip that runs throughout the film is Riggs scuffling through the woods naked. This is a symbolic gesture of defiance against a black community that expects its members to cover and confine the naked truth of individualities based on restrictive notions of black identity. An optimist in the face of adversity, Riggs announces that as long as there is work for him to do and his community needs healing that he will continue living.

My weight and T-cell count are the same...with AIDS you could die...hey...[I'm] wasting my time if I'm not devoting every moment to thinking about how I can communicate to black people, so that we start to look at each other, we start to see each other. (*Black Is . . . Black Ain't*)

Riggs has his say about what black is and ain't because he is invested in a sense of community that can reconcile intracultural difference. He has decided that black people "seeing each other" involves an open communication of difference that has been forsaken in order to insulate a black community that cannot effectively respond to his dis/ease.

Black heterosexism, sexism, colorism, and classism are obstacles articulated in Riggs' personal journey and indicate a great deal about the sources of his personal dis/ease, the larger black community's as well. The responses to Riggs' questions are as eccentric and diverse as his cast—a fact that celebrates intracultural diversity rather than suggesting any failure to pinpoint a collective voice. He makes a powerful but chilling correlation between his dying body and the black community. Statistics at the end of Twentieth Century suggested that AIDS is the number one killer of African Americans between the ages of twenty-five and forty-four. The current rate of HIV transmission shows African Americans vastly overrepresented in new AIDS cases. These facts, coupled with the government's slow response to what has been declared as a State of Emergency in some black communities, is perhaps the biggest threat to black solidarity.[48]

Riggs' *Black Is . . . Black Ain't* optimistically foreshadows the obstacles to a black collectivity that can effectively reconcile difference rather than repudiating it. The necessity of social and political solidarity demands communal healing. Riggs solution is gumbo—a Southern stew that takes all the elements of soul food (seafood, chicken, sausage, and vegetables) and which seizes upon each ingredient's flavor in order to produce a wholesome dish. Gumbo becomes Riggs' hopeful metaphor for the preservation of a shared black sensibility that can reconcile differences in sexuality. If the connection between black people and AIDS is, as Riggs suggests, that both involve a struggle against the odds in the face of possible extinction, then true communion not the flattening out of differences or sweeping taboos under the rug is our 21st Century medicine. Riggs, unfortunately, did not live to

---

48 From 1998 documentary *HIV, AIDS, and African-Americans.* Produced by National Minority AIDS Council in collaboration with the National Institutes of Health and the Office of AIDS Research.

see this gumbo vision actualized. A continuation of this project by those who believe in his legacy and the viability of his vision demonstrates a commitment to a black that not only *is*, but also *is* capable of the healing that Riggs so tirelessly worked towards.

blue-blakk memory

sometimes the gunshots in my ghetto
sound like crack-whips
and at other times
the gentle constant of
"raindrops keep fallin' on my head"
what is in this head of mine
but memories
projected onto futurescapes
sometimes taking my mind to spaces
my body and spirit have
never really known
except through stories
and grandpa's blues?

he said
centuries ago
some resilient and devoted black ancestor
decided to play a little Romeo and Juliet
with the pen and pad
it was a forbidden union
for the black hand pushing the pen to pad
or the black gaze on the white page
could be punishable by death

and I gotta find a way
through this maze of shadow and shade
to somehow
find my way home...

home
the place where I plant these here feet
what is the history of the soil
upon which I stand
sometimes I think that earthquakes
are just agitated spirits
and the floods their tears
shouting when we should cry
and screaming through the earth:
"do not forget me"

sometimes I am a medium
for voices beyond my own recollection
and I be shootin' the breeze
about the current state of dis/ease
and violence
these silences attempt to find
where the mind went
how and where the time was spent
so take me back from hip-hop
to front porches
from pushing a Lex to pushing a plow
like a mule
methinks sometimes we rhyme like fools
forgettin' struggle when we knee-deep in it
feet stuck and mind-struck
'cause we done done too many repetitions of
"we shall overcome…"
but we forgot the urgency associated with it

I'm desensitized and angry
'cause I don't wanna sing that song no more
It's not my song to sing
what ancestral spirit possesses my voice
can somebody tell me
where on earth is my course?

and I gotta find a way
through this maze of shadow and shade
to somehow
find my way home…

memory evoke the presence
of friends and guides
who direct the path that is
no yellow brick road
'cause sometimes having a heart
and a brain, and courage ain't enough still
especially when the wizard
and even the good witch
don't like your color black

so we juba and stomp and praise
we double-dutch and freestyle in our cyphers
make art from the nothing that is everything that is
the know thing that is the evidence
of things not seen
memory sometimes reprimands me
when I forget
when my nostalgia
is but an empty replay
of things learned 'bout
in fictions of texts
so memory
he materialize and come back
and place shackles
on these here black ankles
and we catapult and time travel
into a feel-real pain
no nostalgia can claim or capture
is this my rapture

and I'm running away
I'm running away from
that same black man
I was running away with in memory!
I'm running away
from this same black man
who today
is out to steal my breath!
and I wanna go back in memory
and run away with him
not from him
why don't we remember
when memory could save our lives?

sometimes I wanna remember
wanna go back to when mama's
grandmama's mama
was crossing streams of consciousness
not knowing nothing about what lay
across those other shores
except to know that
it was not the same soil
from which they came

so they cross icy cold waters
dodged gunshots and hunting dogs
for the mere possibility
for the home the follow the feet
across slave plantations
into Jim Crow sting met with a King's dream
the deferred dream of it
wailing in the pain of concrete jungles
and overcrowded ghettos
even in kinder gentler America
we still gotta find a way

through this maze of shadow and shade
to somehow
find my way home

Bodies that (Don't) Matter:
Race, Gender, Sexuality and the Policing of Hip Hop

Keynote presented at Humboldt State University
February 29, 2008

What does it mean to matter?

The most basic definition would define matter as:

mat·ter   (n)
1.   something that is being considered or needs to be dealt with
2.   a substance or material of a particular kind
3.   the material substance of the universe that has mass, occupies space, and is convertible to energy

vi
1.   to be important
2.   to make a difference[49]

I'd like to ponder this latter definition, "to make a difference." It occupies an interesting connation whether one sees oneself as the subject or object of the statement. If I, being an Othered object make a difference, does that mean that I, in fact *matter*, underscoring the potential for agency and mutual recognition. If I am subject, fully endowed with the agency to "make" or "do", then what responsibility do I have to "Others", what can I do to help those on the margins of society, those not empowered or endowed with agency, to achieve full reciprocal recognition. It's an existential dilemma described so well by Sartre and Fanon. The Jew, Sartre believed, was overdetermined because, as an Other, he did not have the ability to engage the anti-Semite on reciprocal terms. Theorist Sonia Kruks suggests that the underpinnings of identity politics have this existential question at center. Marginalized people, as Sartre believe, can take up their Otherness as Pride or Authenticity only insofar as their are defined by those in power as being Others. The authentic Jew is a proud Jew. He or she (re)appropriates their Otherness as a badge of honor and pride. Kruks notes that Fanon went further. The black subject, worse that not being given reciprocal agency by whites, is overdetermined on the outside, leading to a white Negrophobia and, perhaps as damaging, an internalized racism by blacks who accept their place as Other and therefore identify with dominant cultural values, even to their own degradation, even or espe-

---

49 Encarta® World English Dictionary © 1999 Microsoft Corporation. All rights reserved.

cially to their own detriment. The Black, being called out or interpellated as Black by virtue of his or her skin, is devalued upon sight. For Fanon, the historical lineage of Negrophobia creates an especially critical challenge for blacks not wanting to be defined through a negation, but in relationship to his own cultural history and Negitude (or pride in his authentic Africanness subjectivity, not as object). This is relevant insofar as Kruks acknowledges the disjunction between a theoretical idea of reciprocal recognition and the realities that, despite the advances made with regard to racism, its legacy is still very much alive. This Black Pride or Negritude that Fanon references, I then understandable. Who wants to matter only through a negation?

So why does any of existential humdrum "matter"? What does it have to do with queerness and hip hop? What can an existential debate or "identity politics" offer to an understanding of hip hop?

Before delving into hip hop I'll take another liberty and share with you one of my first published poems, which made the collection "Red Dirt Revival" that I wrote as a teen. The piece is called negation. It serves as a positive affirmation of my blackness through identification with my father, though "signifies" that my Black Pride is rooted in his disaffirmation of me (at the time) as a homosexual. It was through not MATTERING because of my queerness, that I had something to prove about my love for blackness, being a man, being tough, keeping it real for real...

(performs "negation" from Breath 1 in Red Dirt Revival)

There's an irony and sarcasm inherent in being TOO black or TOO proud, a critical understanding of the pep talk into a blackness that had denied me on the basis of my homosexuality and that I was trying to, perhaps, overstate. Not just overdetermined on the outside as a black, in the Fanonian sense, I do not have the luxury of being proud even in those spaces where, with other blackfolk, I assume are safe spaces. And it is this awareness that not just my silence, but my blackness, would not protect me, that I've accepted a position as one who becomes more watchful, in those spaces where I'm privileged enough to have agency, to look out for those persons denied it. I want them to matter as much as I matter.

I arrived at Humboldt State University pretty damn excited about being back on campus, not for the first time—drawn her first by my relationship to Eric Rofes and his many interventions on campus to ensure that students, of color and white, queer and straight, male and female and trans, MATTER. I've had a relatively tense relationship to the visits here; perhaps a bit discouraged that there are so few bodies of color in the space than is possible, due to certain Nationalist isolationist ways of being in university that I empathize with, though I have been unapologetically critical of. I was reminded of this when a flyer about this very talk, placed outside of the English dept had the words "Hip Hop is not GAY!!!" written on it.To some on this campus, this public talk, this topic, and my very existence, do not MATTER. And as much as I'd like to shrug off the defamation or disaffirmation of my place in hip hop as an emcee, poet, scholar, as much as I'd like to "man up", keep it "real" and say "fuck it", it hurts a bit. But it also fuels and affirms why I've come to speak. To so many more, I do matter, so I want to thank those who've registered for the class, who'll come to public events associated with the class, and who'll support the work I do beyond this and next weekend.

The audacity of ownership is human. Back in the rural south, where we were growing up, we spoke of something being "minez" or "ourz" (with a z, not as s) as connoting a more passionate claim to something without which we could not live. A student and scholar of English let's call this, the people's passionate possessive or the p cubed. It's the tragic romance of Romeo and Juliet and so many other stories. He was herz and she hiz and that is how it *t.i.iz.* In our civilized world, in our literature and history we are given examples over and again of how tragically human it is for us to want something that is ourz, and the limits to such lustful possessiveness. This might be especially true for those who exist on the margins of society and who feel that there is so little capital or material evidence of their own self-worth. The claim to an ourz might in fact be greater among those who have so little. And it is through this colloquialism that I wish to speak about a fundamental dilemma that is a central dilemma in the hip hop nation, as well as forms of nationalism that exist even here at Humboldt State University.

Consider that you are a disenfranchised person given only certain letters of the alphabet with which to write. You are given limited writing supplies and paper; and only a few books to reference—the select alphabets carefully "x'd" out, so that the privileged can maintain an advantage. A few generations later, your caste of people have devised a very creative, stylized lexicon which enables you to inspire, not just yourselves, but those who selectively provided you the means for your articulation. Now imagine that those in power, in the generations after, decided to claim your language as their own— suggesting that, by default, the master's tools enabled this inspirational language. They mimic and mock it, seldom giving credit to its origination at the margins. This would, I think, be a very dehumanizing and hurtful situation for most. It suggests that certain people don't, in fact, have the right to possess anything, even their own bodies, their humanity, the fruits of the labor. It's harkens back to the institutionalized dehumanization of people of African descent in America for centuries. For all the ways the outcome of creating something of value makes us feel good, there is something human about desiring a claim to those inventions. It's why we have patents. In a capitalist society where the products we produce are almost always assigned a monetary value in the marketplace, p-cubing is as human as the capitalist grip on most of the earth.

Given the necessity of claiming or reclamation, any postmodern claims that hip hop is human music for all people—claims that accentuate its universality while ignoring its origins in the Bronx and among disenfranchised blacks and Latinos—are often met with reasonable resentment and anger by those wanting to claim the music as theirz (and that's with a z). In the face of someone else claiming what is ourz, the boundaries of our creations, our communities, become tighter. It becomes necessary to police these boundaries so that the wrong people don't infiltrate and steal our poetry.

And the problem with this is that, if we can take the liberty of speaking of the hip hop nation as Benedict Anderson speaks of the Nation in his book *Imagined Communities*, is that Nations origin-narratives are not very well served by being porous, flexible, permeable fictions. To be clear, all Nations are rooted in a degree of fiction. England, Japan, Liberia, Russia all work to sustain some unified and coherent and brave narrative of the founding of their nation—though we know there is a lot that is unsaid, left out, and not highlighted, since it would disrupt the purity and romance with the Nation's foundation. So the notion of phantasm is useful here, since there is an element of fantasy inherent in most nationalisms. In America, a picture of the American flag, George Washington, Abe Lincoln, Martin Luther King, or even Hilary or Obama might connote for some the glorious promise of a Nation we should be proud to claim. The sentimentalism of belonging gets even some of the most skeptical of us. Recently, watching Wil-i-am's adaptation of an Obama speech as the "Yes We Can" anthem even struck me a bit emotionally. Yet I've conditioned such sentimentalism to trigger immediate caution against Nationalist propaganda. While I am empathic with and understand the kinds of nationalist unification that keeps the boundaries of disenfranchised people tight and seemingly safe, I vehemently believe that it has to be a means to an end, a point in the journey along a road to a more inclusive way of things and enacting revolutionary practices.

I was introduced to hip hop in Little Rock, Arkansas. Early 80's Grandmaster Flash, Kurtis Blow, roller skating rings in Highland court Little Rock and becoming a b-boy: cardboard breaking and falling in love with this fad called hip hop. We listened to it alongside Madonna, Wham, Culture Club, and Duran Duran, so there was no conflict between love for hip hop and pop, a happy orgy of a bunch of musical strange bedfellows. And what I find ironic about whomever wrote the reprimand on the flyer, is that they, if a student, were not likely even alive when hip hop was introduced to the world, and yet vehemently feel the authority to "police" its boundaries enough to say: Hip Hop is not Gay!!! Well fella or young lady... I have news for you, if you're out there with an ear to the closet door? Hip hop isn't Gay! It's not straight either. It's always already all that and then some. It's Man Parish's Hip Hop Don't Stop and House music deejays paving the path for hip hop deejays who wanted to mix records. Go back and watch Beat Street, Krush Groove, Breakin'. This is not the hard-core, keepin it real hip hop that so many today selectively delete in their romantic imagination of a hip hop that only black and Latino men in the Bronx fell in love with. Yes there were women involved... And yes, some of the men were "faggots."

So to that extent, even as a compulsory silence prevented many of these men and women from coming out, they are as wedded to the origins of hip hop, in their negation, as I am to the blackness my father taught me.

I understand well hip hop's prideful nationalism. As a teenager in racist spaces of rural Arkansas, I did not have the comforts of sheltering by a black ghetto where my interaction with racist whites was rather limited. Here, the beat of a hip hop generation has shifted from creative stories about life in the city to a more politicized discourse about "Fighting the Power." KRS-One, Public Enemy, X-Clan, Poor Righteous Teacher, and Brand Nubian were but a few groups calling for a more purposeful revolutionary intention through hip hop. I was a part of that, helping define and start my own horribly Afrocentrized group as a college student with the acronym DEN (Duke's Enlightened Nubians). I was not out as homosexual, at the onset, but fortunately found a good deal of support around it by my brothas and sistahs in the DEN collective, as long as I remained masculine and didn't remind them that I liked boys. The silence soon got to be too much to bear. By that point I'd been elected president of my school's Black Student Alliance, so found it ironic that the person who'd be seen as most representative of black revolutionary struggle and Nationalism, was allowed to lead, though my queerness was seen as an aberration or distraction from a truer blackness. I continued to do revolutionary work: stopping Privatization on campus due to the affect it would have on black poor and working class employees, organizing and leading a march following the Rodney King verdict, the usual tests of my black allegiance. But as faithful as I'd been to blackness, it was never very faithful to me— failing to have my back when issues related to my sexuality were brought to the fore. So I was betrayed by blackness as well as by hip hop, which, by then, had morphed into a more gangsta, hard-core mainstreaming than I cared for anywhere. Hip hop was dead to me as the affirmation of my queerness came to the fore.

In the reclamation of "real hip hop," that revolutionary stuff that many who embrace today weren't even here to experience, nurtures a misguided fundamentalism. Like a Black Nationalism that faithfully reads selections of Huey Newton or Angela Davis, but never the revisions or updates of the politics of inclusion embraced later, there's a romance with whatever would serve their ability to MATTER. And I empathize with black students and other students of color wanting to MATTER. I don't, however, believe in essentialist politics of exclusion where allies are made to be enemies by virtue of their overdetermined otherness, be it their whiteness or their queerness. There were writings about revolution beyond 1980 and Black Arts Movement. There are old school revolutionaries talking about homophobia, and sexism, and building cross-racial alliances. And unfortunately, it seems that some continue to turn a blind eye to it. People, and especially men of color and white men with something to prove, get to police hip hop against infiltration by fags. I suppose it feels good to MATTER, they become subjects of their own agency, authentic revolutionaries who get to Other Others: "Hip Hop is Not Gay!!!" "Tim'm West does not MATTER." It's the nervous anxiety that hip hop will crumble and fall if we let fags in. And I would suggest that the revolutionary work of hip hop is not a given for even queer bodies who can foster as much violence, sexism, and homophobia as their straight counterparts, in trying to "keep it real" and gain validation. I want the hip hop warriors who, despite their sexual preferences, believe that hip hop can be better. I want emcees and b-boy and girls who understand hip hop's origins as more complicated, diverse, porous, and flexible than many of the hip hop police would like to admit.

(performs "Irony" from the album Blakkboy Blue(s)*)*

I was reading bell hooks' essay "The Coolness of Being Real." I was troubled by here essentializing notions of hip hop as "fake cool" or "fake realness" juxtaposed to a romanticized blues musical aesthetic that she sees as "real cool". Black men who did the blues, in her mind were vulnerable, emotional, and faced the truth of their realities, through their music. Hip hop artists were consumed with a patriarchal masculinity that is an outgrowth of domineering culture and offered little space for "real coolness". After participating in two international- ly acclaimed documentary projects, Alex Hinton's *Pick up the Mic* and Byron Hurt's *Beyond Beats and Rhymes*, I wanted to create a hip hop project that got away from the totalizing views of hip hop as dead where revolutionary work is concerned. There's a lot of good shit out there to listen to. Some of it is coming from queer artists like myself, a lot of it preexists any entry of what has been called Homohop, but is, in fact, hip hop, not a separate codified and therefore dismissive sub- genre. I believe to an extent what hooks says about the vulnerability and "realness" of blues. But I also believe that some blues and jazz brothas were sexist, homophobic men who beat their wives and disre- spected each other. I don't think I'm about romancing any particular genre of music. I also know and have encountered emcees and poets, many or most not queer, who believe in a truly inclusive hip hop where "realness" signifies the presence of men who are involved as full-selves, yes, even if that means that hip hop appears as Gay. I'd like to close with a song. I produced my latest album "Blakkboy Blues" to speak against any dichotomizing of "fake realness" and "real realness". Hip hop can, in fact, be vulnerable and truthful, inclusive and revolutionary, and very good to listen to. I'm no singular savior or disciple of hip hop, but I do believe that there's evidence that the hip hop police (we can call them pigs) will continue to be challenged by those of us wanting a truly authentic hip hop. True in it's difference, in the complex array of personalities and identities drawn to the music, a hip hop that MATTERS and where the subjects drawn to it MATTER.

(closes with "Blakkboy Blue(s)" from the album by the same title)

killin' me[50]

ya'll heteros kill me
you the identity
not even an identity
so normative
you need no nomenclature
and I'm no hater
just an illuminator of truth
and the truth is
y'all killin me!

walking around all day
smilin' and hugged up
public displays of affection
without hateration
without consideration
for what hood you in
or who you gonna offend
for just being you

you hold hands and kiss without care
of how many people will stare
offer prayer
in disgust
so grossed out
they take to public ridicule
of gents with gents
protect the kids
and their pre-adolescent innocence
frustrated common sense

but truth is
y'all needed us
these freakish ways
of lesbian and gays
the spectacle of
bisexuals
marching around
shameless

---

50 "killin' me" originally appeared in *Love In Full Color*, a chapbook created to help fight California's Proposition 8 (2008), which defined marriage as only between one man and one woman.

and being gender benders
transgender
pregnant men
no Adam and Steve
you plead
Nigga please!

see . . . You need us
you were just. . .well. . .
people
before we came along
plain people who could do no wrong
so we make life more exciting for ya
you can gloat about ya favorite scapegoat!
the liberal of you
get to feel proud
it's spoken, "I have a gay friend!"
we ain't trying to be ya token
but sure, I prefer these friendly allies to those
hypocritical believers in churches
acting like they hate us
when the truth is
they need us, desperately
'cause without our sinful ways
their sins would be. . .well. . ."gay"

y'all heteros kill me
you break no rules
you get compliments
for being cute together
picnic baskets in sunny weather
out in broad daylight.
we get reduced to bedroom closets
park bushes and cum deposits
that render nothing but strange fruit
in the garden of good evil
heavy breathing
in dark cities
we are forced to come to
for safety
y'all heterosexuals lazy

don't even give thought to parenting
just check that little test,
smile at your boo
and say
"it's blue!"
or whatever color shows the evidence
of your copulation
we spend years trying to adopt
in states that illegalize our sodomy
deem us a parental catastrophe
so don't talk to me
about putting my sexuality in ya face
your heteronormative oblivion is the disgrace
get outta my face. . .
y'all killin'me   really!
I ain't trying to be silly.

users!
you needed us:
our unorthodox ways
of appropriating the word gay
so you couldn't be happy no mo
without shame
scared to wear jeans too tight
or dance under disco balls at night
life is just so. . . very. . . difficult for you
trying to ignore those of us
dying to be true

but I honor the reality
that heteros gave birth to me
so y'all aiight. . .
sometimes
and sometimes
I'm not even angry
about how you can walk in church
proud to be heterosexual
praying preachers talk about the gays
so they don't have to address
your evil ways. . .

still despite all the ways
ya'll make me sick
I'm glad you exist
will not stoop to tit for tat
or stripping you of your humanity
the insanity that makes our love
some kind of calamity

yeah....some of ya'll okay
'cause for all the ways
this discriminatin' nation makes me wanna hate
even I gotta try to admit:
some of my best friends are straight!

Peep Game[51]

It was 1999
when a nigga across from me at a desk
shed a tear before he gave test
results
I gulped but did not cry
hadn't cried much since I was five
adolescence kissed goodbye.

negative news about being positive
wasn't such positive news
so it intensified my blues

but Peep Game

the beginning of this shit
was the word faggot
was trying to be me
without permission to be free.

I played the games
sweaty b-boy bumps
cipher refrains
fake girlfriends
sexuality maimed
from the basketball courts
to the front porch
I wore a mask
concealing my authenticity
in cities that showed no pity.

Peep Game

pushed down desire
with each fist pound
with every *ay-yo*
with every rebuke of self
my health faded
crept into my psychology

51 Peep Game was originally published in THINK AGAIN © 2003 by New York State Black Gay Network, Inc., and AIDS Project Los Angeles.

cosmology would deem me
a falling star
and no apologies
for living a fraud
just a reminder
every time
I breathe heavy and pause
to redirect my cause.

Peep Game

I took responsibility
for seeking acceptance
between some nigga's arms
and his sweat
and the threats of rejection
by family
by homies
a calamity
so life became lonely
didn't no niggas know me
they knew how I showed me
but when I said *she* I meant *he*
and I stupidly
thought that nigga
was my one and only.

Peep Game

my disease became known
so I could decide to kick its ass
or lay down and die *hella* fast
ironically I finally had
impetus to try
try living life honestly
try being who I was born to be
try being me
the man you see
wanting all y'all to

Peep Game

192 Ts and 33,000 viral load
runny stool and bloody commodes
month long colds
swollen lymph nodes
all hidden by baggy clothes
at the hip hop shows.
I had to come "out" and then "out"
out squared
out square
the ones that called me queer
cuz they didn't care
out rage-us?
fist pounds ain't contagious
the ones I use to give dap
now stand back
and give flack
and say that I ain't a real black.

seems kinda heinous
since they complain about racists.

Peep Game

I'll confess
I digest unpronounceable
and toxic lifesavers
like now or laters
twice daily
feeling crazy 'bout
meds that hurt vital organs
to save my life
but it's all love like the dove
negatives spit negative
but I stay positive
ignoring all the haters
might make my life safer
but It's drainin' as fuck
to always be like: *nigga wha?*
and a neg-a-ro gone go
where the love show.

Peep Game

I overstand Crixivan plans
on empty stomachs
and nightsweats
threats from hets
who try to stress
I get perplexed by HIV activists
tellin' homeless kids
to use condoms
when they ain't got 5 cents
I got beef with agencies
ignoring what's plain to see
and HIV casualties
that take children's families
and handing them a rubber
when they'd rather have their mother
back
and not be black and blue
from abuse and un-truths.

Peep Game

I be trippin' offa sistas
who wanna call niggas faggots
and expect they nigga to tell the truth
if they have it
a word about your reprimand
yo' man ain't so straight
If sexuality's not up for debate
seeing no contradiction
of wanting honesty, integrity
when lips sealed
around the m.i.c. and d.i.c.

But Peep Game

I'm not here to make y'all
paranoid
just to call some shit out
people try to avoid

make noise
and represent
for niggas livin' with this shit
so I got one more beef
and that's it
y'all don't give a fuck about niggas
and yet wanna dictate a nigga dick
that's sick
y'all need to quit.

education programs that vex
'cause they str8 het
teaching only abstinence
this dis/ease is not happenstance
it's a planned redemption
for a life of rebuke
It's seeking shelter inside of somebody

It's getting a disease
some say you deserve
because you dare to find love you deserve
in a swerve.

God bless the stalkers of the night
the men seeking alternatives
to secret lives
God bless the wives
married to these men
God bless the lil' boys
who think their loving is sin
God bless the poems
that fall on deaf ears
ghetto guerilla survival
Eazy E tears
here's to those who scared to find out
here's to those who ain't heard what it's about
here's to those who with each breath
remember the names.

here's to survival

Peep Game.

the dust of skin
(for Eric Rofes)

1.
sturdy shelves held
a few of his books:
the memories collected
i resurrected
like dry bones
forgotten
they were waiting
to be lifted
like his stubborn humility.
reading them now
i hear his voice.
these talking books
offer texture to text
already rich
with purpose.

one day
in search of
lonely pages,
unmarked chapters,
books not read
for all the writing left to do,
paper
not yet peeled back,
stroked,
probed
by the intimacy
of fingertips,
or pupils,
i found him
again.

2.
i realized
that stories spoken,
words remembered
are no less than desire
for connection—

a way we touch the soul.
realized that books
being among the whatevers
we leave behind
for shelves
eventually become
the dust of skin
signify any magic
needlessly forgotten
bound and dense
with language
waiting to be
rediscovered

3.
his books
his flesh
real like the twinkle
in his eye
witnessed over coffee

over projects-in-progress
over sushi in the Castro
or his flirting with life
and so he remains
very much alive
as long as we remember

flashbacks
like re-reads
reveal newness
a deferred intertextuality
a wrestle
with all we wanted to ask
and didn't.

works read
and not yet read
reveal imperfect,
partial conversations.
those of us
who remember

continue to talk with him
each time we read
a letter,
an email,
run across his info
among address contacts,
notice
one of his books
on shelves
again.

some of us
who choose to remember
internalize
his diplomatic scrutiny
perhaps write
and think differently.
'cause he is still editing us
with kind eyes.

4.
and sometimes the people
we grow to love
have already been around
waiting to be touched
if shelved
for a perfect rainy day
or a beach

not unlike my own revival
written with the urgency
of a man dying
though not as fast as feared
someone hopeful
found me and it
so that others could
find themselves.

protected

remind yourself
they are raindrops
heavy
not the sound of him
coming
again
you are not
the blur between 3 and 4
mom and dad didn't leave you here
with him
again
you will breathe easy this time
pillows hold breath
and Jesus loves you
little one

remind yourself
you are 37
can protect yourself
choose the breath beside you
choose who comes to you
with you
on you
if at all
choose the knight
that will protect
from the nightmares

it is the sound
of your heart beating
loud
or rain
not footsteps
anymore
this is Houston
not Dallas
Texas is hot all over
your sweat?
is from that
not a panic attack
like 16

thinkin' the pain
could end if life did

asking Jesus to save you
or forgive
the courage to take a life
tainted
for desiring to be
protected

there is a single tear
for feeling left alone
again
unprotected
remember
you are not a crier
you are a man, no longer a boy
are strong
can kick ass, if needed
sharp knuckles, strong grip,
learned how to box early
knock niggas out
do death grips, find the weak points
for protection

you are 37
strong(er)
can bench press, rap, and basketball
have gotten over fragility
remember you are loved today
there are angels around you
who'd protect if they knew
you get afraid
sometimes
at 37
they will not run away
like disciples at crucifix time
think you are too intense
for bearing truth
the way God has called you to
will stay and protect
when truth gets thick
like tonight

and you are older
and life can smile
like Jesus to a child
if you make it so
hug the pillows tighter
remember
they are big heavy raindrops
and it is the fan blowing
not breath
heavy
some preacher man
telling you to trust God
and breaking your flesh
and spirit
hours after
3 or 4

go back to sleep
write the poem as therapy
about being the real man
you promised to always be
a manly man
a protected protector
by baritone and glare
by swagger and swole
'cause therapists simply make you
feel it all over again
and you have prayed to Jesus
to make you forget

but tonight
the dark feels lonely
and you'd give anything
to be held right
to cry
not for hurting
but because
there are arms
that can make you forget
you were ever 3 or 4
left with a man
of God.

Ruminations of a "Hip Hop Optimist"
An Interview with Tim'm West

By Faedra Chatard Carpenter

This interview was conducted on March 22, 2006, in Washington, DC.

CARPENTER: I know that you are a hip hop artist and that you iden-
tify yourself as a male feminist. Recently, I've spoken to several
women who use the title of "hip hop feminist" to define themselves.
What does that mean to you and would you consider yourself a "hip
hop feminist"?

WEST: Interesting question. I think that I am certainly glad that there
has been that vocalization, with the marriage between hip hop artists
and feminists. There was a time when I was uncomfortable with claim-
ing the title of a feminist because I felt that if there is this exclusive
space where women need to engage and discuss the effects of sexism
and patriarchy on their lives, that as a male claiming that space it cre-
ates a less sacred space for them. I think I got over that because I
realize that the objectives and goals of feminism are not going to hap-
pen without the participation of men. And by disavowing that title, it's
disowning the crucial role a person like me can play in affecting how
people think about sexism. And no where do I see that more prevalent
than in the classroom, as a teacher, with young 15, 16-year-old black
boys and the many ways I get to challenge them daily on the way that
they view women and the way that they process ideas. And sometimes
for the first time in their lives they are in the presence of a black man
who, in a lot of ways, exemplifies what they know a black man to be,
but who, given my thoughts and ideas, really challenges a lot of that. I
hope to open the span of possibilities for the kinds of men that these
young boys will grow up to be, or at least illuminate the possibilities
so that they will have the example of someone who doesn't follow
what they may expect. This is a hip hop generation: a group of young
people who are deeply influenced by hip hop and who know that I am.
It is important to show them that a black man can be critical about the
exploitation of women in hip hop; and also to show them men in hip
hop who aren't falling into that same bandwagon—exposing them to a
larger array of ideas and topics and conversations that can happen in a
hip hop space. So, hip hop feminist? It's sort of a long way to the an-
swer, but I don't know how comfortable I am with that title. I think in
some ways it's sort of similar to feminism for me. I think there needs
to be a space where hip hop feminists who are women talk about what
that means for them. I wouldn't own the title. I'm comfortable with
someone considering me a hip hop feminist, but it's not something that

I would feel comfortable owning right now because I think that there is some kind of developmental space that I want to honor for women who are claiming this. And I simply want them to know…look, I'm your brother, I'm behind you, and I think a lot of the same stuff; but I'm also looking at, you know, getting the brothas together and having some critical conversations among men about sexism.

CARPENTER: You mentioned being a teacher. I know that you perform and lecture on the college and university level, but you also teach high school, right?

WEST: Yes, I have been teaching at Caesar Chavez Public Charter High School for Public Policy. I teach ninth grade English and coach basketball. The age range is anywhere from 14 to 18. And we talk about feminism in my classes.

CARPENTER: And is that the first time your students have heard the term?

WEST: Oh yea, for a lot of them. I wouldn't say for everybody, but for a lot of them it's the first time they've heard "What is a feminist critique?" "What is patriarchy?" And for a school that is predominately youth of color—African American and Latino boys and girls—it's also about introducing these ideas to the young women. And then having these young women of color identify as feminists and talk about Louisa in *Blood Burning Moon* and Jean Toomer's *Cane* or Karintha— talk about these characters in really critical and interesting ways. It's a lot different than the level that you can assume a college student can process and theorize information, but there's something really exciting about planting some of those seeds at the high school level.

CARPENTER: And fundamental and necessary, as well, don't you think?

WEST: Oh, yea.

CARPENTER: I've been talking about these issues with a lot of people in these last couple weeks and the idea of initiating these conversations in our classrooms as early as possible has been raised consistently. From your experience—as a high school teacher—do you think this sort of dialogue and conversation can effectively happen in middle school, in elementary school?

WEST: I think it's going to have to. I think through cultural media, through television and other forms of media, we are introducing a lot of ideas that are assumed to be for adults that young people have access to and yet there is often no context given to those ideas that allows them to really engage and think critically about it. So, they are given a lot of information without the context or conversation about what it means to have—you know—women in a video half-naked, dancing and the connection between that and capitalism. Which is something that you get to introduce at a public policy school. So I think that there are definitely a lot of ideas that do need to happen early and I think that the young people want to know. I think that they are fascinated when you introduce those ideas to them. I think the connection—with the first question you asked about hip hop and feminism—is that feminism, and especially feminist theorizing, has to not become so prudish that it denies a space for that conversation to happen at levels so that working class people, poor people, can understand. So feminism may need to reconsider some of its terms to introduce the conversation. Because we are talking about a hip hop generation. Even as a hip hop artist, I access my whole philosophical lexicon in my rhymes but I also know that most of the people listening to hip hop music are not these high theory cats at universities. So I want the stuff that I write to be penetrable, I want it to be palpable, I want people to be able to grasp and understand it. So yes, I want the feminist ideas to be in the work but I don't want it to be overburdened with so much theory that it's not fun or exciting. So I think that that whole marriage between hip hop and feminism has to have a really critical dialogue about sexism, but in a way that is actually fun. I feel that a lot of where feminism has failed in hip hop is that it is such a dry, "hitting a brick wall" critique, so that it's like, what are some playful, fun ways that sexism has been challenged in hip hop?

CARPENTER: Can you think of any, off the top of your head? Or, can you share with us some ways that you have brought that to the forefront through your music?

WEST: You know, it's interesting because I think this gets in the realm of performance or performance theory, but I think that it's often about the assumptions that we make about people or characters. For example, when we talked in your class about Eminem. There is an extent to which he is duplicating some of the normative hip hop and even sort of the "black masculine" dictates about what a hip hop artist is supposed to be in order to "keep it real." And then there is another side of it that is really playful and I think that Eminem is a little more intelligent than some people may have given him credit for in that he can be playful and he can do drag in his videos and he can sort of talk about this stuff in a way that isn't so serious and, at least, it gets the conversation going. To his credit, there are conversations happening in hip hop maybe as a result of accusations of his homophobia that weren't happening before. This is not to say that that he was deliberate, that it was his intent to shake things up, to be super homophobic to have people talk, but his music is good, it's fun, it's interesting and I think it has to happen in that way. And that's not to say just through the lyrics. I think some feminist criticism in hip hop takes itself too seriously. It loses sight of the fact that people run to this medium of expression because it is uplifting on a certain level and that it is spiritual on a certain level and people connect to the soul of it. You can strip the music of its joy by being too terribly politicized.

CARPENTER: Well, I know that you are an artist of many different genres, but what has drawn you to hip hop and how have you used it for your own messages and social critiques?

WEST: I do a number of things as an artist, but if I were to define myself in one way, I'm a writer. So whether that writing is expressed through poetry, or academic work, or through my rhymes or lyrics, writing is the fundamental focal point. As a young black boy growing up in the eighties and early nineties, hip hop was the medium for people expressing themselves. Some people are like, "What is this queer, feminist black man doing talking about hip hop?", but what else would I talk about? That is all that there was in the culture. To a large extent, [hip hop] would be the medium of expression for someone like me and the fact that I am attracted to men isn't going to somehow deny me that access. It may, in fact, increase it given the homosociality and culture of masculinity and of male-male bonding. It is often a thing I find very interesting and very intriguing, even as it sometimes duplicates the roles of patriarchy and sexism in the culture at-large. For me, it's also like, okay, "I look [hip hop], I sound like that, but I'm not quite that." And that's what's been powerful and interesting for me. I get to embrace aspects of hip hop at at the same time be critical of the culture; something I talk about in my essay, in *Black Cultural Traffic*—

CARPENTER: "Keepin' It Real"—

WEST: Yes, in the "Keepin' It Real" essay I talk about the ways in which disidentification is such a powerful theory because it plays on the identification—the intense identification—with a culture, the "I am hip hop"—you know, "I live and breathe hip hop culture"—but inside that there is some tension, there is some dis/ease, there is a way that the assumptions of an uncomplicated culture underscore the overarching tension that much in hip hop does not really feed me. And, therefore, I have to express that. Every disidentification, the ways in which I distance myself from hip hop, is only because I love it so much. If I didn't love it, I wouldn't care.

CARPENTER: Do you find that you have to fight to create a space as gay, black male hip hop artist or is there a space that you have simply occupied in hip hop? Do you understand what I'm saying? —

WEST: Oh, definitely.

CARPENTER: Because I've heard from other artists and scholars that they don't see a space for feminist discourse in hip hop, but it seems to me that you are making a space for voices that have yet to really be heard.

WEST: That's interesting. I find that somewhat troubling that feminists wouldn't see a space because I think that everything that we've always needed is already there. I think that there are spaces for feminist critique and criticism in hip hop—

CARPENTER: Wait, let me be clear—I don't want to misrepresent. I think most would agree that there is room for feminist critique and criticism, certainly, but is there a place for feminist discourse in hip hop outside of that which reads as a type of critique?

WEST: Oh, I see what you're saying, yea, that's a different question.

CARPENTER: Yes, because if I look at you and I see what you do, what your group does—and we're going to talk about that in a minute—I feel like you are actually *creating* a space to hear new voices. Do you see a space for openly gay and lesbian voices in "mainstream" hip hop or do you think it's going to remain relatively insular?

WEST: Well, I think there is a sort of layered process. For example, if you look at the Homo Hop movement—queers in hip hop, gays and lesbians in hip hop—it starts at a very fundamental level. I know that there is a community out there of other people who are gay, who like hip hop, who are DJs, who are rappers, who are producers, who are b-boys and girls, so the intention is to create a space that is safe for us.

Let's create a space where we can enter a hip hop cipher and freestyle and no one is going to trip out if I talk about drama with my boyfriend. Because there is a certain thing about hip hop and the improvisational nature of it that is connected to our jazz tradition. I mean, what if a jazz musician—similarly, because the language of the medium for the articulation in hip hop is the voice—what if the voice of the trumpet had to stop or pause every time the articulation of its feeling was "gay"? Well, fortunately, with music you don't have that same issue. It's not language, so you don't have that same tension. But when it's hip hop and it's words and it's very bluntly talking about experience and you can't do so as freely as you might imagine, then it becomes inauthentic art. It's an art that's not authentic in terms of it's not living up to hip hop's rootedness in creative expression about one's experience.

So, of course, there needs to be a space to talk about sexuality in hip hop. So, let's do it. And that initially may mean bringing together, or collecting, or mobilizing other queer hip hop artists. The world we live in isn't insular and so I think we always knew, in those early years, when we were sort of having these little conferences and having hip hop concerts and bringing people from around the world together for a weekend at a time to do stuff, that in our individual circles, we are simultaneously interacting with straight guys and straight girls and so it's going to move, it's going to translate over and translate to, maybe, the black "assumed-straight" world. It's going to also translate over to a gay culture that has largely seen hip hop as an immediate threat to everything that it stands for. And if you look at the white, gay power structure, hip hop is scary to them because it's urban black men expressing their discontent with the system in a lot of cases or expressing in general. And for a lot of white gays that's like, "What does that have to do with me?" It's forcing a lot of conversations about those spaces in-between.

I think feminism is all the better because queers are doing hip hop. It explodes the dichotomous framing of a male/female dynamic; especially if a female rapper can diss a male rapper by calling him a punk or a sissy, then it becomes more complicated than women being assertive when she is indirectly and ultimately berating the feminine. Or, if two gay rappers can sit around and call each other punk or faggot or sissy as an insult, it's not even about the body or the identity of the person delivering, but a certain illicit code. It goes back to me to the master's tool question. Can you use hip hop, these tools, these turntables, and this freestylin' and all these forms that are associated with hip hop, when it's simultaeously forging notions of an urban, hypermasculine patriarchy? There was an article I was reading the other day about "post hip hop" and there are people who completely disidentify with hip hop, therefore, they create this other term. And I was really uncomfortable with the whole "post hip hop" thing.

CARPENTER: Tell me more about that, why?

WEST: Well, it spoke to people who are just sort of tired with the increasing "blingism" and obsession with money and violence and all of those negative things that have been associated with hip hop if you are a backpacker, conscious, hip hop personality.

CARPENTER: What do you think is lost with the term "post hip hop"?

WEST: We disconnect, we create another term, and I think—maybe as a postmodernist on some kind of level—I always assume that there is going to be some inadequacy with whatever we create. So, yea, we've done that before: we've created a new term and then we realize that it's inherently flawed. And one of the things I tried to do theoretically in the "Keepin' It Real" essay was to try to be self-critical of my own artistic creations. I'm in this rap group, Deep Dickollective, it started in the Bay area, to a large extent by black, feminist-minded, queer male, critique/theory-oriented guys who wanted to do some smart, intelligent, witty hip hop. And we did, as a joke, and it kind of blew up and then it's like, we're going to be Grand Marshals at the San Diego Pride Parade this summer on a damn float! A black, queer, dreadlocked, nappy-headed group of guys and we're probably going to be the only black people there (laughs), but you know that speaks volumes about how things have shifted. But, back to the idea of "post hip hop"…

CARPENTER: Well, do you think it was conceived to denote an evolution of the material and/or genre?

WEST: It's a delusional disidentification. It attempts to disidentify with hip hop in language, but when you talk post hip hop, it's still hip hop. So, I guess there may be two models that you work in that system to change and shift it. Or you work outside and you say we need something altogether different, but then when you look at what's different, is it really? Is that difference something that can happen successfully inside? And maybe it's the whole Martin Luther King/Malcolm X dichotomy when you say "Fuck the system" and we're going to do this on our own versus the idea that we're going to work within the system to try to create changes. There was this artist featured in a documentary film I'm in called *Pick Up the Mic*. One of the guys talks about how he had this idea that he called "Pulling a Melissa Etheridge," which I thought was really funny. His whole thing was that he was going to do this straight boy hip hop thing, land a big deal, do a couple of albums, closeted, and then pull a Melissa Etheridge, you know, "Okay, you all like me, I'm dope, Now what?!" But he got outed before he got to pull his Melissa Etheridge, lost his first record deal, lost a lot of his fans, and was then sort of forced to embrace this community of openly gay hip hop artists. And for a while it was really tense because I think he saw himself as being validated by the straight people as good. He saw homo hoppers as "other" hip hop, but over time I think he realized, no this *is* hip hop. This is a community of people who are doing hip hop.

And yes, there are gay hip hop artists that I don't think are that great, but there are straight hip hop artists that I don't think are that great, so it's not about the orientation as opposed to the quality of the message. There are gay hip hop artists that perpetuate sexism and patriarchy in their lyrics, probably less so than the average, run-of-the-mill straight hip hop group, but it's not about just being gay or straight. What's going to happen if in "post hip hop" you still find the same issues of patriarchy and sexism and homophobia? Are you going to do post-post hip hop? You can continually run away from the thing itself or you can accept the thing itself as inherently flawed and have this self-reflexive, conscientious understanding about the ways in which the medium fails to really be inclusive and hold everybody respectfully. So, I'm all about claiming hip hop. I mention the term "Homo Hop," which I actually created as a joke, but I did it tongue-in-cheek and poking fun, and a journalist picked it up and the next thing you know it's a mention in the *New York Times*, and I was like, you know it was a joke, right? But I think the shortsightedness around terms like homo hop or post hip hop is that you deny hip hop's potentiality, as it exists, to be self-critical and to be progressive and to change itself. But by creating a new category, you are basically denying that hip hop has that power to heal itself, to be inclusive.

CARPENTER: So do you regret having that term, "Homo Hop," leaked out?

WEST: Well, it wasn't intended to create a whole, separate hip hop genre. It's interesting because I think *Pick Up the Mic* at one point was going to be something like *It's Homo Hop* or something crazy like that; and I really like that they went with *Pick Up the Mic* so that if you saw the poster and read the title, you'd just think it was a movie about hip hop—

CARPENTER: And then it does "A Melissa Etheridge"—

WEST: Right! And then it does a Melissa Etheridge and people go in the theatres and go, "Oh!"

CARPENTER: So now that the term *is* out, can "Homo Hop" be used in an empowering way?

WEST: I think so, but I think it has a specific place in the sense of talking about that earlier idea of mobilization. It's like "hip hop feminist," right? They need to have that space to distinguish themselves. But the problem I have with that, I guess, is that there have been hip hop feminists since day one. So are you then denying the history and legacy of feminism in hip hop in ways where the people are not necessarily identifying as such, but there is certainly the critique going on, there were certainly challenges to sexism happening all along. For example, Queen Latifah's "Who you callin' a bitch?" before there was any term such as "hip hop feminist." I don't want to deny that history. Or Man Parish and what's it called? "Hip Hop Don't Stop"? An eighties hip hop track done by a gay man. I don't want to deny that history by suggesting that all of a sudden it's the late nineties and we have this thing called Homo Hop. No, we've been in the mix for a while. So, you need that distinction on a certain level, but by creating these terms, if you take it too seriously, I think you deny the potential for the thing itself to be dynamic in the way that it already is, right? Hip hop always already has, built inside of it, the possibility for critique. One of the things I love about Foucault's notion of power is that power is always vulnerable, it always already is, so you don't have to go outside of it to find the holes—they are already there.

CARPENTER: Looking at the commercial side of hip hop and the possibilities of that, how have you and your group, Deep Dickollective, been able been able to appeal to other audiences? Do you see a future for gay hip hop artists appealing to "mainstream" audiences without having to "pull the Melissa Etheridge"?

WEST: Well, I think D/DC is a very interesting case to look at because on stage and even sonically, we sound like backpacker hip hop boys. We are masculine, black men, dreadlocked, have Afrocentric sensibilities. There have been many cases where we've performed alongside Biz Markie or Spearhead or another sort of Afrocentric, black hip hop crew and people didn't even pick up on the fact that we're queer because they hear the beats, they see the people on stage, they see the mics passing and the freestylin and then after the fact it's like, "Oh." And I think that sometimes it's unsettling because it's like, "Oh, they're gay!" And we are these people who are not supposed to be in hip hop, but they just saw it and it sounded just like hip hop.

CARPENTER: But those are the revolutionary moments, right?

WEST: Yes, those are critical revolutionary moments and sometimes they happen through a refrain in a song like, "Queer boys doing hip hop is a revolutionary act. Queer girls doing hip hop is a revolutionary act" and having that be something that you start doing in a crowd and people start chanting. Or, just—how beautiful and wonderful language is!—how you can take words or quotes that may have been intended to be used in a certain way and recontextualize them so that they actually become queered in a sense. So when Common, in one of his earlier albums, says, "In a circle of faggots your name is mentioned" and it was intended to be a diss against another straight rapper, when a gay rapper says "In a circle of faggots my name is mentioned," it's like bragging rights! So you're reappropriating the diss. So yes, the homophobia is there, the sexism is there, but it already has holes. How can we expose the holes, how can we collectively work to expose the volatility?

CARPENTER: As you're talking, you consistently remind me of how interdependent the issues of sexism and homophobia are. So why is there such a gap in the dialogue? Why hasn't this been a more pronounced and active conversation between those who wish to dismantle these ideologies?

WEST: I think to some extent [aligning patriarchy and heterosexism] becomes a "crab in the barrel" situation. Because we've worked so hard and so long to address feminism in hip hop to sort of add on this gay issue seems too murky or complicated. You know, "let's deal with one issue at a time." And you know, there are also probably hip hop feminists who may feel somewhat threatened by this other thing and they may feel that we haven't really fully addressed sexism, so why are we going to move on to the next thing? So I think it's about seeing the intersections. That's why it's really hard for me to talk about homophobia in hip hop without talking about sexism. It's also about capitalism, about a market, about how you sell things, but if you look at indie hip hop, independent artists, the realm of possibilities that have exploded with internet media, the fact that a whole community of people could come together online should generate some optimism. Most of us in the so-called "Homo Hop Movement" found each other by typing "gay hip hop" or "gays in hip hop" in a Google search engine.

CARPENTER: That was a while back, what comes up now?

WEST: Well now, of course, there's gayhiphop.com which is like one of the central sites, but if you type in "gay hip hop" now you are going to get several, several, several, several, pages of artists and people who are talking about it, but at one point you'd put it in and you might find one thing here or one thing there and many of those would be homophobic references, not really a positive mentioning of "gay and hip hop." And I think just the fact that there's more out there is a form of resistance. You don't have to rely on getting signed or getting a record deal to get your product out there and to have people listen to you. D/DC have done college tours, we've done big shows at festivals, we've produced CDs, we sell our CDs at shows and online, so I think on some level technology has helped to create and opened a space for the types of voices that people can hear. People aren't necessarily going to say, "Well if I don't get a deal I can't do my work," because now people can have a home studio and create almost as good an album as somebody at a big studio. So on some level the playing field has been leveled and therefore a lot of the people that aren't getting the deals because maybe they do have voices or opinions that aren't considered marketable by mainstream standards have access to present their work in other ways... But there are some real barriers in hip hop. And if we only create these alternative spaces, and create these safe spaces, and don't infiltrate and interweave ourselves into the mainstream, then it denies the potential for hip hop to heal itself. If we are going to say that hip hop is this dis/eased body, that hip hop has the potential and agents to fight the disease, how do we do that?

CARPENTER: It's a huge question, but do you have any possible answers?

WEST: I think we need to look at what currently exists in hip hop for the voices that are trying to say something different. I think often hip hop feminism and critiques often focus on what is wrong and they don't look enough at what's right, or what's clever, or what's interesting.

CARPENTER: So, that comes back to being creative and being fun.

WEST: Yea, I'm one of these people who wants to listen to Lil' Kim's album. I don't want to take for granted that she's some sort of lost soul, doesn't want to be a black girl, doesn't want to exercise her own power, wants to wear skimpy clothes. I want to listen to that and be critical of her, but I don't want to dismiss her or assume that she doesn't have the potential to contribute something that might be healing to hip hop.

CARPENTER: Do you see hip hop lasting another thirty, sixty years?

WEST: I do, that's why I don't think we need a post hip hop. Hip hop is already post hip hop. Just like "post-feminism." I've also heard "post-Black." I have the same reaction to that as well. What are we claiming when we say "post"? Post-modern I get because it's a very distinctive shift in the way of thinking about something. If it's going to be post-feminism, then it better be damned different from the original.

CARPENTER: I want to back up a bit and talk about your own relationship with hip hop and when and how you began to see the possibilities of hip hop.

WEST: For me I think a real critical turning point was when I began to see voices that I didn't initially imagine as part of the hip hop community actually being able to speak. When I first saw women rap, I remember getting excited about that because that said to me that hip hop could change. When I first saw white rappers—I was a huge Beastie Boys fan—

CARPENTER: Was this before you were actually rapping yourself?

WEST: The Beastie Boys have a lot to do with why I started rapping (laughs)—

CARPENTER: Really?!

WEST: It wasn't so much that I wasn't interested in rapping before, but I had a pretty early awareness that I was queer and I just thought that there was really no space for gay people in hip hop. So all of a sudden when you see these Jewish boys from Brooklyn rappin' alongside LL Cool J or Run DMC and it's like...maybe there is that possibility for that change. Then you see a Monie Love or a Queen Latifah talkin' about "Ladies First" you say, yes, there is potential for that change. I think hip hop has everything it already needs. Maybe it's as simple as a glass half-empty and half-full. And maybe I'm just a hip hop optimist. Maybe it's all about understanding that what we need is already there and learning how to engage with what's already there more critically. Let's not assume that there isn't something more complex going on with these dirty south rappers with dreadlocks and gold teeth. Yes, there is this tension with expressing this Afrocentric aesthetic and a Bling aesthetic but let's not just dismiss that. Let's look at that. Let's engage and have dialogue with the people that are promoting that. I think that far too often the assumptions and accusations are made and no one is communicating. So maybe that's it—maybe I'm a hip hop optimist. Maybe that's the term I need to use.

Faedra Chatard Carpenter (B.A., Spelman College; M.A. Washington University; Ph.D. Stanford University) is a freelance dramaturg and an assistant professor of theater and performance studies at the University of Maryland, College Park. A former resident dramaturg for both Arena Stage in Washington, D.C., and Crossroads Theatre Company in New Jersey, Carpenter has also worked as a professional dramaturg for Center Stage, The John F. Kennedy Center for the Performing Arts, the African Continuum Theatre Company, Theater J, Black Women Playwrights Group, and TheatreWorks. She is a member of the Board of Directors for Literary Managers and Dramaturgs of the Americas (LMDA), an Advisory Editor in Drama for *Callaloo: A Journal of African Diaspora Arts and Letters*, and an Editorial Board Member for *The Southern Quarterly*. Carpenter's scholarly interests include the study of race, sexuality, and gender in contemporary performance and her work is published in *The Cambridge Companion to African American Theatre*; *Review: The Journal of Dramaturgy*; *Theatre Topics*; *Women & Performance*; *Text and Performance Quarterly,* and *Callaloo*. Carpenter's manuscript *Coloring Whiteness: Black Performances of Critique* is under contract with The University of Michigan Press.

prognosis
(for my father, Bishop C.E. West)

ready pops?
ready to tackle this?
this space between you and me
called home?

every letter I have written
is the anthology of you
begetting me
becoming you
to lose you
become me
in the pull and tug
of refinement

we stumble and fall
we cradle and kiss
we Wests
lovers of God
saviors to children and the meek
justice champions
memoir writers
renegade bad boys
church boy / heathens
baritone thick
bellies full
bull-strong and fearless
charisma blessed
sinner-saints

blood lines
like blood memory
is how we carry this prognosis
body ignoring the inevitability
of what becomes
when you hold too much.
I am a run-tell-all
to save myself
from the disease of shame
that has chained you.

I release truth as surely as you
wield scripture to believers
as painfully as you
never forgive what God already has

maybe this prognosis
that burns my eyes
for knowing this day would come
prophetic
and prepared
to be your rock
Gibraltar-like
black and strong
is what we have always needed
to see each other
purely

will you promise to know
you are forgiven
by me
if not by your self
for I, too, am a man of God?
will you remember
through this fight
that I ain't lived for nothing but
making a country Kentucky-born marine
BlackIndian, lover-boy, preacher-man
proud?
boxing gloves and cleats
books and bible
in the falling hard and hurting hard
the talking through our silence

I am your son
imperfect and whole
invested in the blind faith
of recovery against odds
scientific
in the exactness
and methodology of prayer
and miracles

remember pops?
at 2 or 3
I fell asleep on your belly
you snored
I slobbered
we woke to church and Jesus
Holy Ghost and Project bullets
basketball and slap-boxing
survival for the fittest
so you taught
roll and duck
jab and tackle
pray hard(er)...
for this day
would come

prognosis
hangs in the balance
of our prayer and fight
we WESTS

ready pops?
ready to tackle this?
this space between you and me
called home?

toast

I propose a toast
for all the times
I forget you
not meaning to.
feeling so well
so often
I forget...
without you?
there is no me at all
I'd wither and die
return to dust
like I almost did
before you came
to rescue

a toast
for I have been a Judas
preferring to deny
or hide you...
not wanting to be denied
loneliness cloaked in muscle
fear guised by baritone
not wanting to face another
"you're the perfect guy for me...
but..."
not wanting to embody
the irony
be somebody's
imperfect perfect
ever again

a toast
for there are times
I simply can't stomach you
moments
teary-eyed
when you don't go down
easy
but we manage

flavor the water with color
carbonate to cut through
this necessary toxicity
that heals me
makes my cells stronger
quiets the enemy
killing me softly.

a toast
for the resistance
you build
when I break our vow
seek a vacation, unsanctioned
overwhelmed
by this bond
begat by bonding.
never wanting to need
anything
like this...
I have failed you
with deliberate carelessness
embraced my liberation
my strident independence
and you always accept me back
if changed
if I promise to do better
and I always do

a toast
a bottled water
and you, held in hand
colorful and delicate
more powerful than shame
raised to my lips
at noon, and midnight
this daily kiss and make up
we do
will someday end
but today...
a toast
for outlasting
the loves that brought us

together
the loves that promise
to stay
but don't
my truth
the most alluring part of me
yet always too much to bare

so I will always
take you quickly
to shorten the moment
the memory
that I would die
without you
that I don't wanna die
 alone
don't wanna remember
this remnant
of a broken trust
or broken lust
so I thank you
this painful gratitude
is necessary
is the demonstration of will
and fight

for someday
you'll help me get
what I desire
another
who'll abide
with us both
shamelessly
help me manage you
better...
this, my love,
is what I live for:
you and me
so often seeming
incomplete.

with full breath
and all the strength
my spirit can muster
for you
and us
a toast
for hope
for life.

About the Author

Tim'm T. West is a poet, scholar, rapper, and youth activist who was born in Cincinnati and raised primarily in rural Arkansas. A contemporary Renaissance man, he is a featured voice in many documentaries about hip hop and masculinity because of his groundbreaking work as a gay-identified hip hop artist, AIDS activist, and youth advocate, among other affiliations. A teacher and cultural producer at a number of secondary and post-secondary institutions, as well as a former varsity basketball coach, West has a B.A. from Duke University and graduate degrees from The New School for Social Research and Stanford University. He is author of several books (*Red Dirt Revival: a poetic memoir in 6 Breaths*, *BARE: notes from a porchdweller, Flirting,* and the forthcoming *pre|dispositions*), is widely anthologized, and also has produced and released nine hip hop albums, the first several with iconic queer rap group D/DC. In 2013 he released his fifth solo project, *snapshots*. Tim'm West travels and lectures widely and recently served as Director of Youth Programs at Center On Halsted in Chicago.